OAT
CUISINE

OAT
CUISINE

Pamela Westland

Salem House
Manchester, New Hampshire

© Ward Lock Limited 1985

First published in the United States by Salem
House Publications, 1986,
a member of the Merrimack Publishers' Circle,
Manchester, New Hampshire 03101

ISBN: 0-88162-167-6

LIBRARY OF CONGRESS CATALOG CARD
NUMBER: 85-72575

Text filmset in Novarese
by Dorchester Typesetting

Printed and bound in Spain by Cayfosa, Barcelona
Dep. Leg. B - 28808-1985

Contents

Notes

All spoon measures are level.

All recipes serve four people unless otherwise specified.

Acknowledgements

Food photography   Grant Symon
Home Economist   Jane Suthering
Stylist   Penny Markham

Oats for photography provided by Quaker Oats Limited, England.

Introduction

What's in an oat? How much is packed into that insignificant-looking little grain? The answer, I suspect, is more than one would think.

First and foremost, there's survival on a great scale, for cereals alone still support and nourish half the world, and across several continents and over thousands of years oats have played their part. The seed has germinated and flourished in soils too poor, too wet and too cold to play host to other, less hardy grains. And so oats have reached parts of the world where, generations ago, other cereals could not reach.

Then there's nutritional value. The next chapter outlines the direction in which modern medical research is pointing. To tell us something that Britons — yes, it has to be said, the Scots and the Welsh particularly — North Americans, Scandinavians and other Northern and Eastern Europeans seem always to have known: that oats are good for you. *How* good, is the subject of continuing and immensely rewarding research. To say that the soluble fiber content of oats has been found actually to be an effective treatment in severe cases of diabetes and high blood cholesterol is to put it in a nutshell. And to indicate that a daily intake of oats can be an effective preventive measure in these and other ailments.

And then there's flavor. No other cereal tastes like oats. There's that slightly sweet, slightly sour taste that I have likened to "dry yogurt". There's a depth to the flavor that prevents it from being bland — and that should help to keep eager fingers away from the sugar bowl.

And there's adaptability. With fresh and dried fruits, in baked goods and desserts, oats seem the perfect "sweet" accompaniment. With vegetables, cheese, fish and meat they seem the natural partner to savory dishes. And blended with other grains — with whole wheat flour in pastry and bread, for example, oats really prove that, in terms of flavor, they have the dominant genes. Moreover, they are in many ways interchangeable. You can, for example, equally well toss herrings in rolled oats or any grade of oatmeal, and fill them with a herb mixture based on cooked groats, oatmeal or rolled oats. To thicken sauces you can use fine or medium oatmeal, oat bran or oat flour, and in baking you can vary the texture according to whether you use oatmeal or rolled oats.

Last, but very closely linked with all the other factors, there's tradition. Whole nations have been programmed, deep within their cultures, to sit companionably around the breakfast table savoring the warmth and satisfaction of a bowl of steaming porridge. And now new generations, still faithful to the grain, are following the lead of the Swiss physician, Dr. Bircher-Benner, and making that nutritious and companionable bowl one of muesli. The recipe that he devised early this century, it is worth recalling, was for rolled oats, raw apple, lemon juice, hazelnuts and milk. And that, he averred, constituted a perfectly balanced meal.

Since I began writing this book, people have said to me, "But isn't it terribly dull? Doesn't the food all taste the same?" With chapters on breakfast dishes, snacks, soups and casseroles, main dishes, accompaniments, desserts and baking, I haven't found it the least bit dull to write.

As to all the food tasting the same, well there's a world of difference, it seems to me, between, for example, mushroom pâté and lemon soup; carrot crumble and leeks in white wine; spiced lentil pilaf and pheasant packed with herbed oatmeal; summer pudding and banana tea bread; oatcakes and cheese and herb bread. But you must be the judge.

Full of Goodness

Oats have never suffered at the hands of the diet fads and fancies that have beset other foods; the about-faces of being recommended by an impressive string of experts one year, only to be declared completely taboo the next. No, oats have always enjoyed the reputation of being "good for you", though it is only very recently that medical research has advanced to the point where this instinctive knowledge can be well substantiated.

One of the reasons for this health-image consistency is that oats, unlike wheat, have not fallen victim to food technology. They have not had the "goodness" milled out of them and been offered for sale in a refined and abused state, as high-rise flour and light-as-air processed foods. Actually, they couldn't be, for oats are very low in gluten. This means that the flour milled from them will not rise in baking, with or without the bran. So almost certainly it is this natural deficiency which has saved them from the clutches of the food do-badders. They have had, perforce, to leave oats where they have always been – as groats, rolled, flaked, cut or ground, but nutritionally *complete*.

THE COMPOSITION OF THE GRAIN

When oats are harvested, the panicle, or frond, consists of stalks that hold the oat kernel inside the outer husk, or chaff. The whole oat remains when the chaff has been winnowed away. To the farmer this grain is the seed for the following year's crop. To the food manufacturer the whole oat is the raw material that forms the basis of all oat cereal products.

Each grain consists of an outer coating which comprises the bran, endosperm and germ, or embryo. In wheat, it is the bran and much of the germ that are processed out to leave an incomplete and nutritionally diminished product – white flour.

Whole oats contain (according to a standard work on the composition of foods*) 72.8 per cent carbohydrate, which is essential for body energy; 12.4 per cent protein, which is needed for growth; 8.7 per cent fat, balanced between polyunsaturated and saturated fatty acids, and significant amounts of potassium, magnesium, calcium and phosphorus.

Studying the vitamin content of oats gives a reassuring nutritional picture. Go to work on a bowl of oats and you provide your body with the get-up-and-go of vitamin B_1, *thiamine*, which serves to convert carbohydrates into energy in both muscles and nervous system; B_2, *riboflavin*, which, together with oxygen, is needed by the body to convert into energy amino acids from proteins, fatty acids from fats, and sugars from starches, to produce and repair body tissues and maintain healthy mucus surfaces; *niacin*, one of the vitamin B complex, which also helps to produce energy from carbohydrates, fats and proteins, and is essential for the correct functioning of the brain and nerves and the maintenance of healthy skin, tongue and digestive organs. Also present in that cereal bowl is vitamin B_6, *pyridoxine*, and vitamin E, *tocopherol*. What oats do not contain, however, is vitamin C, at least not until the germination process is begun and they are sprouted – see page 77 for the simple-as-child's-play instructions.

THE FIBER STORY

So much for the nutritional element of the grain. But what of that non-nutritional yet vitally beneficial component so much in the news these days, the dietary fiber? It is in this area that much recent medical research has been concentrated, and which has produced some revealing and – medically speaking – exciting facts.

A team of researchers at Kentucky University, led by Dr. James Anderson, has been isolating the different properties of the two distinct types of dietary fiber present in the cell walls of plants. One type, easily recognizable in the dry-as-dust form of wheat bran, for example, is termed water-insoluble. The other, known as soluble fiber, can be identified as the sticky, gummy substance in oats that makes a nonstick pan almost a "must" when making porridge, and as the slippery, translucent substance that forms a protective coating around tomato seeds.

All plants contain some dietary fiber, and of both types, but it is found in greatly differing

*McCance and Widdowson's *The Composition of Foods. Fourth revised edition by A. A. Paul and D. A. T. Southgate. Published by Her Majesty's Stationery Office, Great Britain.*

proportions. Wheat and nuts have more insoluble than soluble fiber, while oats, barley and rye are good sources of the water-soluble type.

Lack of dietary fiber in the Western diet, due to the preponderence of refined and non-plant foods, has made our society prone to a long list of ailments, many of them killers. It is no coincidence that the illnesses are collectively referred to as "Western diseases". They include coronary heart disease, the commonest cause of death; cancer of the large bowel; appendicitis and diverticular disease of the colon – the most common disorders of the intestine; gallstones; obesity; diabetes; hemorrhoids; varicose veins and tooth decay. A formidable list indeed!

The properties of water-insoluble fiber such as wheat bran are well-known after the welter of publicity given in recent years to high-fiber diets. This type of fiber acts as roughage, bulks up the waste materials in the body, and speeds their passage through the digestive system.

Soluble fiber, which swells as it absorbs water in the intestine, carries sugars further down the bowel before they are absorbed, and also, it seems, delays the process of emptying the stomach. This has the secondary effect of curbing the anticipation of the next snack or meal.

Slow-release foods

With the latest research findings, new phrases are creeping into our vocabulary. We learn that some foods high in fiber are termed "slow-release foods", and that they are a good thing. It has been found that whole grains of all kinds – wheat grains, brown rice and others – products such as whole wheat semolina and pasta which are made from coarsely ground grains (as distinct from bread, which is made from finely ground flour), and soluble fiber all help other foods present in the intestine to release their energy components slowly. This is the very reverse, clearly, of sugar, which is a quick-release food and often deprecatingly dubbed empty calories.

In addition, a decade of medical trials by Dr. Anderson has produced evidence that *beta glucan*, the soluble fiber found in cereals, has helped to control and reduce harmful levels of sugar and cholesterol in the blood.

This has been of particular benefit to sufferers from diabetes, which is commonly caused by an excess of sugar in the blood, created by the body's inability to control the balance between its own sugar production and the sugars consumed. Dr. Anderson's high carbohydrate/fiber diet, based on the soluble fiber in oats, has meant that many patients have been able to give up the standard insulin treatment entirely and others to reduce their intake considerably.

The same medical team has found that harmful cholesterol levels in men show a reduction of some 20 per cent after a diet supplemented by oat bran. Since it is the build-up of excess cholesterol which can lead to hardening and eventual blockage of the arteries and heart valves, the value of these findings cannot be overestimated.

THE CALORIE COUNT

Many people who, without perhaps being able to quote chapter and verse, have never doubted the nutritional and other health advantages of oats, do, however, harbor suspicions on one point. The myth lingers that oats, whether they are enjoyed raw as muesli, cooked as porridge or served in any other way, are fattening, which is, to put it mildly, unfair.

Assume that a 1oz serving of oats or oatmeal contains about 95 Kcalories and you have to admit that whatever else it is in the cereal bowl that makes you fat, it isn't going to be the grain. Take a bowl of crunchy muesli or a steaming plate of porridge, however, and stir in generous amounts of nuts, dried fruits, whole milk or yogurt and even the smallest amounts of sugar or honey, and you pile on the calories. But don't blame the oats!

It is not, however, only in terms of their own limited calorific value that oats can contribute to a slimming or weight maintenance program. In common with all high-fiber foods, they have the effect of reducing hunger by invoking a feeling of fullness and meal satisfaction. That way they play an important part in the psychology of slimming, or what may be termed "food intake control".

In short, a bowl of oats for breakfast *instead* of a plate of sausages, egg and bacon, or a main course or dessert made with oats, instead of cholesterol-rich or harmful sweet ingredients, will both avoid any temptation to embark on a calorific binge and, eaten regularly, will also provide the basis for a healthy diet, and moreover, one that is rich in flavor and texture.

Shopping Around

The increasing present-day popularity of oats must represent one of the most remarkable marketing phenomena of all time. It can't often come about that a product known to have been around for several thousand years suddenly attracts a massive surge of interest and enjoys a sales boom. It isn't, after all, these days, as if we are low on choice. There was a time when oats were the staple food of whole countries and parts of continents for no better reason than that they, above all other cereals, grew there most readily, in the prevailing climate and soil conditions. Not so now. With improved, more hardy strains of other cereals, and modern transport and communications systems, stores are packed with as wide a choice as one could wish for – ranging between brown rice, golden cornmeal, cracked wheat, rye flour, barley flakes and buckwheat to name just a few among them.

No, it must have something to do with the distinctive, slightly sweet, slightly sour flavor; quite a bit to do with the versatility in cooking of all kinds, and a great deal to do with their health-maintaining properties, that oats are experiencing such a thrust of product loyalty.

FROM FIELD TO TABLE

Six producing nations split up 75 per cent of the world's annual oat crop: the United States, USSR, Canada, Poland, Germany and France. The remainder is produced in the United Kingdom, Denmark, Sweden, Czechoslovakia, Australia and Argentina.

In some countries, the seed is usually sown in the spring and combine-harvested in August and September, weighing in at the mill with a moisture content of around 16 per cent. It is then cleaned and graded, then sifted and kiln-dried. In this, perhaps the most important of the processes, the grains are partially toasted by currents of hot air, to emerge with a moisture content reduced to 6-7 per cent, and with the sealed-in characteristic flavor and aroma of the oat.

After more cleaning and grading, the grains are hulled and then, in the age-old winnowing process, the tough, light outer husks are blown away. This at last reveals the oat groat, which is the whole grain, almost cylindrical in shape, blunt at the germ end and pointed at the "beard" end.

From this point the groats are subject to different processes, depending upon the form in which they are destined to appear on the store shelves.

Stabilization

If you have ever come across an oat product that smelled rancid or tasted bitter, then it probably had not undergone an extra heat or steam treatment. An enzyme present in the grain, *lipase*, converts the natural oil to glycerine and fatty acids which, though important to plant development, result in deterioration in flavor in the ungerminated grain. The heat treatment which is part of the rolling and flaking process – to manufacture rolled oats – kills this enzyme. Oatmeal of all grades, plus oat bran and oat germ, all need heat-stabilizing.

Types of oat products

The whole grain oat is processed to produce several distinctly different though often interchangeable forms of oats.

When you are shopping, there is no substitute for reading the labels. Only then can you be sure you buy what you want to buy.

Oat groats

As mentioned earlier, these are the complete, whole grain oats. They resemble long-grain brown rice to some extent in appearance and, indeed, in use, and are available mainly through health-food shops.

Jumbo oats

These round, flat rolled oats, the largest of the oat products, are descriptively named. They are produced from the whole oat grain, steam-treated to stabilize and soften it, then lightly rolled. The oats are of uniform size, creamy white flecked with brown, and familiar as the firm, dry, crunchy ingredient in muesli.

Rolled oats and oat flakes

Smaller than jumbo oats though otherwise similar in appearance, rolled oats, also called oat flakes, are made from coarse oatmeal. The oatmeal is first steamed to deactivate the enzymes, then passed through heavy rollers to crush and flatten it. The rolled oats are highly versatile and can be used in everything from crumble toppings to salad dressings, bread to baked vegetable fillings.

Oatmeal

There are three main grades of oatmeal – *steel-cut*, which is the coarsest, followed by *medium* and *fine*. All are produced by cutting the oat groats.

Steel-cut oatmeal looks like exactly what it is, the whole processed grain neatly chopped into three. It is best soaked overnight and then simmered in soups, casseroles, fruit dishes and, of course, porridge.

Medium and fine grades of oatmeal are made by further reducing the cut oats by means of rollers. They are excellent thickening agents and, unlike coarse oatmeal, can be added to dry baked goods such as breads and pastry.

Oat flour

Not widely available, oat flour is cut to a very fine texture. It can easily be made at home by grinding jumbo oats, rolled oats or oatmeal in a blender or food processor. Alternatively, fine oatmeal can be substituted.

Oat bran

Produced with a high content of outer seed casing, or bran, of finely ground groats, it is the bran which contains the highest concentration of soluble fiber in the grain. It is available in health-food stores as an individual product, or packaged under a brand name as oat bran and oat germ – the germ being the kernel of the grain. These products are stabilized for ensured quality, and can be added to bread, scone and pastry mixtures, fillings, toppings and muesli, in addition to being sprinkled over soups and desserts.

Packaged cereals

There are a number of ready-packaged breakfast cereals competing for the mighty porridge and "instant hot cereals" space on the supermarket shelves.

Some are simply jumbo oats or rolled oats packaged with the manufacturer's quality guarantee. Some rolled oats have been partly precooked to cut down on precious breakfast-time minutes; others, known as instant oats, consist of flakes mixed with oat flour. Yet others have added vitamins, iron, wheat bran, sugar or salt. The permutations are seemingly endless.

Varying your Oats

You could sit down at breakfast in Denmark to a plate of raw oatmeal sprinkled with milk and sugar – the forerunner of muesli?; move on to Finland for a taste of oat kissel, a creamy whole grain dessert served with butter and herbs or spices; spoon up a dauntingly thick onion and oat soup in France; down a refreshing and restorative glass of oats and water in Africa; share a nutritionally boosted meat and oat casserole with a Muslim family preparing for Ramadan; and be approached on a visit to Pakistan, where the grain has a high currency value, by a black marketeer saying "Psst! Want to buy a can of rolled oats?" For oats certainly get around the globe.

No one knows when and where the first wild oats grew. Oats are known to have been under cultivation, in plants bred from the wild, in the Near East in 2500 BC, and traced on Iron Age sites in Asia. Virgil wasn't a member of the oats fan club – he "had but little esteem" of them, but generally the Greeks and Romans recognized their nutritional and culinary value. And so oats, in company with so many plants, made the trek across Europe and went everywhere the Romans went. Which made sense, for the advancing armies colonized some places with pretty cool, wet climates, and their oats just thrived and thrived.

THE POPULARITY OF PORRIDGE
The Scots, who had firmly established oats alongside barley as a staple cereal crop by the 13th century, claim porridge as their own. There are other claimants too: the Vikings set great store by it; in Ireland, and Wales where it is called brewis, people have been going to work on it for hundreds of years; in Norway they serve it with sour cream; and in West Africa it carries the reputation of giving power and health to young and old. In the Northern United States, another region where the inclemency of the climate is an open invitation for oats to flourish, *their* porridge is made by combining coarse oatmeal with water and eating it raw.

PORRIDGE OATS
Purists may not agree, but porridge doesn't *have* to be oatmeal or rolled oats simmered to a creamy consistency, and nothing else. A bowl of porridge has the potential for as many variations as a muesli mix. Whether you choose coarse oatmeal, jumbo oats, rolled oats or, indeed, a mixture, the flavoring variations are endless.

Try a sweet and sour dressing of lemon or orange juice and a drizzle of honey; a cored and chopped dessert apple tossed with ground ginger, cinnamon or grated nutmeg; sliced banana tossed in lemon juice and shredded coconut; a handful of dried fruit and nuts; a floaty layer of wafer-thin dried banana "chips"; or, slightly more eccentric perhaps, 1 tablespoon chopped parsley, marjoram, mint or thyme stirred into each portion of porridge.

Just as the Nigerians do, you can make a nutritious drink by stirring 1-2 tablespoons of medium oatmeal or rolled oats into a glass of iced water or chilled skim milk. Try further variations, using unsweetened fruit juice such as apple, pineapple, orange, black currant or raspberry, and, if possible, including a slice or two of fruit. Stir oatmeal or rolled oats into a glass of chilled fruit purée, thinned down, if needed, with milk or buttermilk, and sprinkle a few toasted oats or nuts on top. Served with one or two oat cakes, it's a meal in itself.

Oats blended variously with grated cheese, low-calorie cottage cheese, chopped nuts and rubbed-in low-cholesterol margarine make deliciously golden savory and sweet crumble toppings for vegetables, fish, meat and fruit dishes. The Romans gave us the idea – they had a delicious creamy chicken dish with an oat crumble topping and dreamy oat-topped cheesecake. Scone dough with the pleasantly sour flavor of oats makes a hearty cobbler topping. And, with the low proportion of fat to flour, and no sugar, scones are among the healthiest baked goods you can find.

NOT-SO-LEAVENED BREAD
The poor rising properties of oats mean that baked goods have to compensate in terms of flavor for what they lack in lightness. The Welsh get around this problem by disguising the chewy toughness of Siot, an oat cake, by dipping it in buttermilk.

Oats give a deliciously "different" flavor to breads if fine oatmeal or oat flour are blended with whole wheat flour in the proportion of, say, one to four for wheat bread with an oat flavor, and in the proportion of one (oats) to two (wheat flour) for a flatter, heavier but deliciously oatier loaf; or if jumbo or rolled oats are added to bread and scone doughs, and tea bread mixtures, thereby giving both crunch and bite.

For a powdery topping, a dusting of fine oatmeal is ideal on baked goods; and, moving up the scale, crunch can be provided by coarse oatmeal, rolled oats and oat groats.

A HANDFUL OF OATS
Straight from the jar, a handful of oats is quicker than making bread crumbs as the basis for fish, poultry and meat stuffings, or to coat whole fish or chicken and veal scallops.

Cut down on saturated fat – housekeeping money too – by "extending" ground meat in sauces for pasta, vegetable fillings – stuffed eggplant or peppers maybe – and meat loaves by stirring in oatmeal or rolled oats. After all, that's what the Scots do in haggis, that controversial mixture of organ meats, oatmeal and lard, and skirlie, or mealie pudding, a type of white sausage.

Oats do a good job of soaking up fruit juice or thickening stewed fruit, and can be scattered over a pastry base to keep it from becoming soggy.

Use oat flour or, just as effective and my own preference, fine oatmeal, for thickening sweet and savory sauces, gravy, soups and casseroles. Providing you stir it in immediately and constantly, oatmeal, unlike wheat flour, will blend into a sauce without needing the liaison of fat.

The texture of jumbo oats, particularly, and rolled oats gives a real lift to salads of all kinds, tossed, perhaps, with apples, celery and dried fruits with a yogurt and lemon dressing. Alternatively, the oats can form part of the dressing, tossed with the vinaigrette ingredients or blended to a smooth sauce.

TOASTED OATS
Topping a recipe with toasted oats adds lots of crunch and few calories. All that needs to be done is to broil the oats on a baking sheet under moderate heat for 3-4 minutes, stirring often.

GROATS, THE ULTIMATE OATS
The whole oat grain, or oat groats, need to be soaked overnight, then dried before being cooked for 1¼-1½ hours in a large pan of boiling water or stock. Drain again after cooking.

Alternatively, the soaked and drained groats can be cooked as follows:
Oven: Heat a large ovenproof dish of water to the boiling point, then add the groats, cover and bake in a moderately hot oven, 375°F, for 1¾-2 hours.
Microwave oven: Cook the groats and enough liquid to cover on HIGH for 14-16 minutes.
Slow cooker: Boil the groats in a large pan of liquid for 20 minutes, then transfer to a preheated slow cooker, and cook on HIGH for 8 hours.
Pressure cooker: Cook the groats for 20-35 minutes at HIGH pressure in 2 inches of water.

Once cooked, groats have the appearance and many of the characteristics of long-grain brown rice, and can be used in salads, risottos, pilafs, rissoles, stuffings and soups. As with other long, slow-cooking ingredients (legumes for instance), it makes sense to cook more than your immediate needs so that you have some ready at hand for all the other uses. They store perfectly in a lidded container in the refrigerator, or can be open frozen, then stored in a sealed plastic bag for up to 6 months.

PORRIDGE – BASIC COOKING METHODS

The thickness of porridge is a matter of personal taste. Proportions are best gauged by volume, in the proportion of one of oats to two-three of water or other liquid.

Cooking method	Rolled oats	Jumbo oats	Coarse oatmeal	Medium oatmeal	Fine oatmeal
Direct heat	Heat oats and liquid to boiling point, then boil for 1 minute. Remove from heat. Set aside for 5 minutes.	Heat oats and liquid to boiling point, then simmer for 10 minutes.	Soak oatmeal in water overnight, then heat to boiling point, and simmer for 40-60 minutes.	Soak oatmeal in water overnight, then heat to boiling point, and simmer for 15-20 minutes.	Heat oatmeal and liquid to boiling point, then simmer for 2 minutes.
Double boiler	Heat oats and liquid to boiling point, then cook for 10 minutes.	Heat oats and liquid to boiling point, then cook for 20 minutes.	Soak oatmeal in water overnight, then heat to boiling point, and cook for 1-1¼ hours.	Soak oatmeal in water overnight, then heat to boiling point, and cook for 30-40 minutes.	Heat oatmeal and liquid to boiling point, then cook for 5 minutes.
Oven	Heat water to boiling point, then add oats, cover and cook in a hot oven, 400°F, for 10-15 minutes.	Heat water to boiling point, then add oats, cover and cook in a hot oven, 400°F, for 20-25 minutes.	Heat water to boiling point, then add oatmeal, cover and cook in a hot oven, 400°F, for 40-50 minutes.	Heat water to boiling point, then add oatmeal, cover and cook in a hot oven, 400°F, for 20-25 minutes.	Heat water to boiling point, then add oatmeal, cover and cook in a hot oven, 400°F, for 10-15 minutes.
Microwave oven	Cook the oats and liquid on HIGH for 4 minutes.	Cook the oats and liquid on HIGH for 5½-6 minutes.	Leave oatmeal and liquid to stand for 2-3 hours, then cook on HIGH for 7-8 minutes. Stir or whisk vigorously before serving.	Cook oatmeal and liquid on HIGH for 3½-4 minutes, stirring vigorously, then cook for an additional 3½-4 minutes.	Cook oatmeal and liquid on HIGH for 2-2½ minutes, stirring vigorously, then cook for an additional 2-2½ minutes.
Slow cooker	Heat oats and liquid to boiling point in a pan, then transfer to a preheated slow cooker, and cook on LOW for 8 hours.	Heat oats and liquid to boiling point in a pan, then transfer to a preheated slow cooker, and cook on LOW for 8 hours.	Soak oatmeal in water overnight, then heat to boiling point in a pan, and boil for 3 minutes. Transfer to a preheated slow cooker, and cook on LOW for 8 hours.	Soak oatmeal in water overnight, then heat to boiling point in a pan. Transfer to a preheated slow cooker, and cook on LOW for 8 hours.	Heat oatmeal and liquid to boiling point in a pan, then transfer to a preheated slow cooker, and cook on LOW for 8 hours.
Vacuum flask or insulated covered container	Heat oats and liquid to boiling point. Transfer to flask or other container. Cover, set aside for 1 hour, or overnight.	Heat oats and liquid to boiling point. Transfer to flask or other container. Cover, set aside for 1 hour, or overnight.	Heat oatmeal and liquid to boiling point, then boil for 5 minutes. Transfer to flask or other container. Cover, set aside for 2 hours, or overnight.	Heat oatmeal and liquid to boiling point, then boil for 5 minutes. Transfer to flask or other container. Cover, set aside for 1½ hours, or overnight.	Heat oatmeal and liquid to boiling point, then boil for 5 minutes. Transfer to flask or other container. Cover, set aside for 1 hour, or overnight.

Hello, Sunshine!

People in Northern Europe have been going to work on a bowl of oats for centuries. In Scotland, it is made from oatmeal, and stirred, almost ritually, with a wooden stick called a spurtle. There they eat it well-salted and unsweetened, and dipped, spoon by spoon, into a bowl of milk; not swimming in hot or cold milk and sprinkled with honey or dried fruits, as the English tend to prefer it.

Perhaps our ancestors knew by instinct what medical research now shows – that oats are a good source of protein and carbohydrates, and are relatively low in fat and calories. A great way to put vigor into the day and to enjoy also at all times.

Health food enthusiasts have been giving the cereal a popularity boom, since jumbo oats and rolled oats are the main basic ingredients of muesli, to which you can add your own choice of seeds, nuts, fresh and dried fruits and even vegetables.

But don't stop there! Oats make a tasty and nutritious addition to yogurt, milk and fruit shakes; a deliciously sticky topping for broiled grapefruit; a crisp and crunchy "jacket" for broiled fish, and a crumbly textured biscuit to serve with savory dishes or cheese.

SCOTS PORRIDGE

4 oz medium **or** coarse oatmeal
3¾ cups water
salt

Put the oatmeal and water into a small pan, stir well, cover and leave to soak overnight.

Add the salt, and heat slowly to the boiling point stirring all the time. Simmer for 15-20 minutes if using medium oatmeal and for 40-60 minutes for coarse oatmeal. Stir occasionally. Serve at once, in heated bowls.

Note The traditional Scots way is to dip a spoonful of porridge into an individual bowl of cold milk, and to sprinkle more salt over it. In other regions, porridge is served with hot or cold milk poured onto it, and sweetened with honey or brown sugar.

To cook different types of oats, see opposite.

FRUITY PORRIDGE

1 cup rolled oats **or** jumbo oats
3¾ cups water
salt
3 tablespoons lowfat yogurt

2 tablespoons golden raisins
2 tablespoons currants
8 dried apricots, chopped
2 tablespoons Brazil nuts, chopped

Put the oats and water into a small pan, stir well, cover and leave to soak overnight.
Add the salt, and heat slowly to the boiling point, stirring all the time. Simmer for 10 minutes, stirring occasionally. Remove from the heat and beat in the yogurt, then stir in the dried fruits and nuts. Serve at once, in heated bowls.
Serve with milk, buttermilk or more yogurt.

MUESLI BASE

MAKES 4¾ cups

2½ cups rolled oats
½ cup jumbo oats
½ scant cup oat bran and oat germ
6 tablespoons sunflower seeds
1 cup chopped mixed nuts

Mix together all the ingredients. Store in an airtight container in a cool place.

Note The muesli base will keep for several months if stored as above.

FRESH FRUIT MUESLI

SERVES 2

1 dessert apple, pared, cored and chopped
1 orange, divided into segments, pith and skin removed
1 banana, thinly sliced
juice of 1 orange
½ cup Muesli base
2-4 tablespoons berries, hulled and picked over, e.g., blackberries or strawberries
(optional)

Toss the apple, orange and banana in the orange juice. Put the muesli into serving bowls, and scatter the berries on top, if used.
Serve with skim milk, buttermilk, lowfat yogurt or unsweetened fruit juice.

DRIED FRUIT MUESLI

1 cup Muesli base (page 16)
6 tablespoons dried
apricots, chopped
2 small dried figs, chopped
3 tablespoons dried banana "chips"

⅓ cup dried pitted dates, chopped
⅓ cup golden raisins
2½ tablespoons mixed
candied peel, chopped
juice of 1 lemon

Mix together the muesli and dried fruits. Sprinkle each serving with lemon juice, and serve with skim milk, buttermilk, lowfat yogurt or unsweetened fruit juice.

Note The dry mixture can be stored in an airtight container.

VEGETABLE MUESLI

SERVES 2

⅓ cup dried pitted dates, chopped
1 medium carrot, grated
2 stalks tender celery, thinly sliced
¾ cup button mushrooms, thinly sliced
½ small bulb fennel, thinly sliced, if available
1 tablespoon pumpkin seeds
½ cup Muesli base (page 16)

Stir the fruit, vegetables and pumpkin seeds into the muesli.
    Serve with buttermilk or lowfat yogurt.

Note To save time in the morning, the vegetables can be prepared overnight and stored in a small, lidded container in the refrigerator.

TOASTED MUESLI

SERVES 12

1 recipe Muesli base (page 16)
7 tablespoons shredded coconut
4 tablespoons clear honey
2 tablespoons sunflower oil
⅔ cup seedless raisins

Mix the muesli and coconut. Melt the honey and oil in a pan, pour this over the muesli, and mix well. Spread the mixture on baking sheets. Bake in a moderately slow oven, 325°F, for 25 minutes until browned, turning the mixture frequently with a wooden spoon so that it cooks evenly. Cool completely, then stir in the raisins.
    Serve with skim milk, buttermilk or lowfat yogurt.

Note Store the dry mixture in a lidded container in a cool place.

MORNING COCKTAIL

¾ cup rolled oats
1¼ cups skim milk
6 tablespoons dried
apricots, chopped
⅔ cup water
2 bananas, sliced
1 dessert apple, pared, cored and
chopped

juice of 1½ oranges
1 teaspoon grated orange rind
½ cup hazelnuts

DECORATION

orange wedges

Soak the oats in the milk overnight. Soak the chopped apricots in the water overnight.

Purée the oats, milk, apricots, water, bananas, apple, orange juice and orange rind and the hazelnuts in a blender, or press the apricots and banana through a sieve, grate the apple, finely chop the nuts and mix together all the ingredients. Pour into four glasses, and serve with orange wedges.

PEACH SUNDAY

SERVES 3-4

⅓ cup medium oatmeal
1¼ cups lowfat yogurt
⅔ cup unsweetened pineapple juice
3 fresh peaches, skinned, pitted and chopped
2 eggs

DECORATION

2 tablespoons rolled oats, toasted

Stir the oatmeal into the yogurt, cover and chill in the refrigerator overnight.

Purée the oatmeal, yogurt, pineapple juice, chopped peaches and eggs in a blender, or sieve the peaches, whisk the eggs lightly, and mix together all the ingredients. Pour the mixture into glasses, and sprinkle with the toasted oats. Stir, if desired, into the mixture just before drinking.

Variations
Other fresh fruits, according to season, can be substituted for the peaches.

OPPOSITE *Morning Cocktail*

FIRST-DOWN COOKIES

MAKES 12

⅓ cup medium oatmeal
⅔ cup milk
⅓ cup dried pitted dates, finely chopped
2 tablespoons hot water

½ scant cup oat bran and oat germ
1½ cups whole wheat flour
1 tablespoon sunflower oil
½ cup golden raisins
1 dessert apple, pared, cored and grated

Soak the oatmeal in the milk for 30 minutes. Soak the dates in the hot water for 30 minutes, then mash them to a paste. Stir in the oatmeal and milk.

Mix together the oat bran and the flour, then stir in the oatmeal mixture and the remaining ingredients. Spread into a well-greased 7 × 11 inch pan, and level the surface. Bake in a moderate oven, 350°F, for 20-25 minutes until golden-brown. Mark into 12 fingers, and leave to cool slightly in the pan. Cut out and cool on a wire rack. Store in an airtight container.

Note These cookies make a nutritious start to the day combined with an apple or orange.

OAT CAKES

MAKES 16

2 cups rolled oats **or** jumbo oats **plus** extra for rolling
1 cup whole wheat flour
salt
1 teaspoon baking powder
4 tablespoons sunflower margarine

Mix together the oats, flour, salt and baking powder. Rub in the margarine, and sprinkle with just enough water to make a firm dough.

Scatter some oats over a working surface, and knead the dough lightly. Roll it to a circle about 7 inches in diameter and ¼ inch thick. Using a plate as a guide, trim the dough into a neat circle. Re-roll to form a second circle.

Place each dough circle on a greased baking sheet, and cut into eight wedges. Bake in a moderate oven, 350°F, for 25 minutes until browned at the edges. Leave to cool slightly in the pan, then transfer to a wire rack. Serve spread with lowfat cheese and dried fruits.

OATMEAL BANNOCKS

MAKES 4

⅔ cup medium oatmeal **plus** extra for rolling
a pinch of baking soda
salt
2 teaspoons sunflower margarine, melted
oil for greasing

Mix together the oatmeal, baking soda and the salt. Stir in the margarine, then sprinkle on just enough hot water to make a stiff paste. Form the dough into a ball.

Scatter oatmeal over a working surface, and knead the dough lightly. Roll it to a circle about ¼ inch thick. Using a plate as a guide, trim the dough to a neat circle, then cut it into quarters. Sprinkle a little oatmeal on top.

Cook the bannocks on a hot, lightly greased griddle or in a heavy skillet over high heat for 3-4 minutes until the edges start to curl. Place under a moderate broiler, and cook until the bannocks are crisp.

Serve hot or cold, with fish.

POTATO HOTCAKES

SERVES 2

2 lb potatoes, peeled and grated
2 tablespoons medium
oatmeal
2 tablespoons rolled
oats **or** jumbo oats

1 small onion, grated
1 teaspoon dry English mustard
salt, freshly ground pepper
2 eggs, beaten
oil for greasing

Put the grated potato into a colander and press out the moisture, using a saucer. Alternatively, wring the potato in a clean tea towel.

Mix the potato with the oatmeal, rolled oats, onion, mustard, salt and pepper. Beat in the eggs to form a thick paste consistency.

Drop heaping tablespoons of the mixture onto a lightly greased griddle or heavy skillet, and fry over moderate heat for 2-3 minutes on each side until the hotcakes are evenly brown. Serve hot, with fish or broiled mushrooms and tomatoes.

STUFFED MUSHROOMS

1 lb button mushrooms
2 tablespoons olive oil
1 tablespoon sunflower margarine
1 small onion, finely chopped
⅓ cup medium oatmeal

2 tablespoons chopped parsley
2 tablespoons chopped walnuts
salt, freshly ground pepper
4 tablespoons lowfat cream cheese

Pull out the mushroom caps and chop the stalks. Melt the oil and margarine in a pan, and fry the onion over moderate heat for 3 minutes, stirring occasionally. Stir in the chopped mushroom stalks, the oatmeal, parsley and walnuts, and season with salt and pepper. Beat in the cheese, then remove from the heat.

Place the mushrooms caps in a greased baking dish, hollow side up. Divide the filling between them, pressing it well into the caps. Bake in a moderately hot oven, 375°F, for 15-20 minutes until the filling is bubbling. Serve at once, with toast and, if desired, halved tomatoes baked in the oven at the same time.

BROILED GRAPEFRUIT

4 grapefruit, halved and cut into sections
1 tablespoon seedless raisins
a pinch of ground ginger
4 tablespoons rolled oats
1 tablespoon clear honey, melted
2 tablespoons orange juice

Place the grapefruit, cut sides up, on the broiler pan. Press the raisins into the cavity left after removing the central core.

Mix together the ginger, oats, honey and orange juice in a bowl, and spread the mixture over the grapefruit. Broil the grapefruit under moderate heat until the topping is brown and crisp. Serve at once.

Oat Cakes (see page 20) go well with this hot and tangy breakfast dish.

OPPOSITE *Grilled Herrings* and *Oat Cakes* (*page* 20)

BROILED HERRINGS

4 fresh herrings, heads removed, gutted
and cleaned
2 tablespoons lemon juice
salt, freshly ground pepper
2 tablespoons fine oatmeal
2 tablespoons sunflower oil
2 tablespoons French mustard

⅓ cup rolled oats **or** jumbo oats
4 tablespoons sunflower
margarine, melted

GARNISH

lemon slices
dill sprigs

Sprinkle the inside of the herrings with lemon juice, and season with salt and pepper. Toss the fish in the fine oatmeal to coat them.

Brush the fish with the oil, and broil under high heat for 3 minutes on each side. Brush with the mustard, then press on the oats to coat them. Sprinkle with half the melted margarine. Broil again for 3 minutes, turn the fish, sprinkle with the remaining margarine, and broil for an additional 3-4 minutes. Garnish with the lemon slices and dill. Serve at once, with Oat Cakes (see page 20).

——Time is the Essence——

Everyone's so incredibly busy these days. I am forever hearing people say that they haven't time to prepare and cook a meal because of this commitment or that. And, what's more, that there's scarcely time to grab something to eat before dashing out again. Which, of course, simply won't do!

But there's no denying the fact that the fast-food era is upon us. And even in the best regulated of households there are bound to be times when a quick single-course meal is the order of the day.

Quite unlike the other chapters, this section is a scrapbook of ideas for quick snacks and easy appetizers. Some of the recipes you can prepare in advance and leave ready to eat in a hurry, others you can whip up when you're more interested in having something tasty to eat, soon, than in the actual therapy of cooking.

Oats really come into their own at times like this. They add valuable nutrients and soluble – easily digestible – fiber, proving that the terms "fast food" and "junk food" are certainly not synonymous.

In pâtés, dips and savory fillings, oatmeal is a useful extender, diluting strong flavors in the way that bread crumbs do; but spooned straight from the package, it's a good deal quicker. In egg dishes, oats can add both bulk and texture – they're amazingly good in pancakes – and help you produce satisfying dishes with a reduced cholesterol level. And in salads, especially the kind that make a meal, oats have just what it takes – crunch and eye appeal.

WIDE-OPEN SANDWICHES

MAKES 4

2 medium bananas, mashed
2 tablespoons fine oatmeal
⅓ cup dried pitted dates, chopped
8 dried apricots, soaked, drained and chopped
4 teaspoons lemon juice

4 slices Oat Bread (page 92)
I dessert apple, cored and thinly sliced
I peach, skinned, pitted and thinly sliced

GARNISH

watercress sprigs

Mix together the bananas, oatmeal, dates, apricots and half the lemon juice. Spread the mixture over one side of each slice of bread.

Toss the apple and peach slices in the remaining lemon juice, and arrange the fruit over the banana filling. Garnish with watercress.

Variations

Top the basic sandwich with other fresh fruits in season, e.g., raspberries, blackberries, sliced plums or pears.

STUFFED TOMATOES

4 large tomatoes

STUFFING

2 tablespoons sunflower oil
1 medium onion, finely chopped
2 cloves garlic, crushed
1 green pepper, seeded and finely chopped

1½ cups button mushrooms, chopped
1 cup chopped mixed nuts
½ cup whole wheat bread crumbs
½ cup rolled oats
2 tablespoons chopped parsley
salt, freshly ground pepper

Cut a thin slice from the top of each tomato. Use a teaspoon to scoop out and reserve the seeds, taking care not to pierce the "walls". Stand the tomatoes upside down to drain.

Meanwhile, make the stuffing. Heat the oil in a pan, and cook the onion and garlic over moderate heat, stirring occasionally. Add the pepper, reserved tomato seeds and mushrooms, stir well and fry for 2 minutes. Stir in the nuts, bread crumbs and oats, and stir over the heat for 1 minute. Remove from the heat, stir in the parsley, and season with salt and pepper.

Stand the tomatoes in a baking dish. Spoon in the stuffing, and press it down firmly. Bake in a moderately hot oven, 375°F, for 25-30 minutes until bubbling. Serve hot.

Serve with a green or dried bean salad.

MOUNTAIN OMELET

SERVES 2

1 tablespoon sunflower oil
1 medium onion, chopped
1 clove garlic, crushed
2 small zucchini, diced
2 small cooked potatoes, peeled and diced
2 tomatoes, skinned and chopped

3 eggs
1 tablespoon water
6 tablespoons rolled oats
salt, freshly ground pepper
a pinch of cayenne pepper
2 tablespoons grated Edam cheese

Heat the oil in an omelet pan, then fry the onion, garlic, zucchini and potatoes over moderate heat for 3 minutes, stirring frequently. Stir in the tomatoes.

Beat the eggs with the water, then stir in 4 tablespoons of the oats. Season with salt, pepper and the cayenne pepper. Pour the egg mixture into the pan, and stir lightly with a fork. Cook until the base of the omelet is just set and the top is still moist.

Mix the cheese with the remainder of the oats. Sprinkle over the omelet, and broil it under moderate heat for about 30 seconds, to set the top. Serve at once, with a salad. Alternatively turn it onto a plate, and leave to cool.

Note Cut into wedges and wrapped in foil, the cold omelet makes a good lunch-box alternative to sandwiches.

MUSHROOM SCRAMBLE

SERVES 3-4

¾ lb button mushrooms
2 tablespoons olive oil
2 tablespoons orange juice
1 teaspoon grated orange rind
⅔ cup dry cider
3 tablespoons red wine

2 cloves garlic, finely chopped
1 bay leaf
salt, freshly ground pepper
2 large tomatoes, skinned and chopped
2 tablespoons fine oatmeal
2 tablespoons chopped parsley

Trim the mushroom stalks level with the cap. (You can use the stalks in soup or a sauce.)
  Put the oil, orange juice and orange rind, the cider, wine, garlic and bay leaf into a pan, and heat to the boiling point. Season with salt and pepper, then simmer for 5 minutes. Add the mushrooms, and simmer for 5 minutes. Stir in the tomatoes and oatmeal, and simmer for an additional 3 minutes. Season to taste, then stir in the parsley. Serve warm, with whole wheat bread.

MUSHROOM PÂTÉ

2 tablespoons sunflower margarine
2 small onions, chopped
2 cloves garlic, crushed
½ lb field mushrooms, chopped
⅔ cup cottage cheese
¼ cup medium oatmeal
1 teaspoon soy sauce

1 tablespoon medium sherry
salt, freshly ground pepper
2 tablespoons chopped parsley

DECORATION

mushroom slices

Melt the margarine in a pan, and cook the onion and garlic over moderate heat for 3 minutes, stirring occasionally. Add the mushrooms, stir well, then lower the heat. Continue frying for 10 minutes, stirring frequently, then lift them out with a slotted spoon.
  Put the vegetables in a blender with the cheese, oatmeal, soy sauce and sherry, and process until the purée is smooth. Alternatively, press the vegetables and cheese through a sieve, and mix with the remaining ingredients. Season the purée with salt and pepper, then stir in the parsley. Spoon it into four individual ramekin dishes, and level the surface. Cover with plastic wrap, and chill overnight in the refrigerator. Garnish with the mushroom slices.

OPPOSITE *Mushroom Pâté* and *Cheese and Nut Pâté*

CHEESE AND NUT PÂTÉ

SERVES 6-8

1 cup lowfat cream cheese
½ cup toasted hazelnuts, coarsely ground
⅓ cup medium oatmeal
2 tablespoons chopped parsley
1 medium carrot, grated
1 stalk of tender celery, finely chopped

½ small green pepper, seeded and finely
chopped
2 scallions, finely chopped
salt, freshly ground pepper

GARNISH

watercress sprigs

Mix together all the ingredients, and season to taste with salt and pepper. Press the mixture into a dish, and level the surface. Cover with foil, and chill for 2 hours or overnight. Garnish with the watercress sprigs.

Serve with whole wheat crackers or toast.

Variation
Pack the pâté into seeded peppers, wrap them in foil, and chill. Serve thinly sliced, as an unusual first course.

27

LAYERED SALAD

SERVES 4-6

½ cup rolled oats **or** jumbo oats
6 tablespoons sunflower seeds
⅓ cup dried pitted dates, sliced
6 tablespoons dried apricots, sliced
3 tablespoons currants
½ small red cabbage, thinly sliced
2 medium carrots, grated
2 small onions, sliced into rings
1 red pepper, seeded and thinly sliced

1 green pepper, seeded and thinly sliced
2 dessert apples, cored and thinly sliced

DRESSING

4 tablespoons olive oil
4 scallions, finely chopped
2 tablespoons unsweetened
pineapple juice
salt, freshly ground pepper

Mix together the oats, sunflower seeds, dates, apricots and currants, and set aside. Mix together the dressing ingredients until well-blended.

In a bowl – a glass one is ideal – make layers of cabbage and carrots, cabbage and onion rings, cabbage and pepper, cabbage and apples, then finally a layer of cabbage. Sprinkle the oat mixture between each layer. Pour the dressing over the salad, but do not toss it.

Serve with whole wheat rolls spread with cottage cheese.

VEGETABLE MEDLEY

2 tablespoons sunflower margarine
2 tablespoons sunflower oil
2 medium onions, thinly sliced
2 medium leeks, thinly sliced
2 medium carrots, thinly sliced
2 medium zucchini, sliced
2 large tomatoes, skinned and sliced

½ cup jumbo oats
1¼ cups chicken **or** vegetable stock
⅓ cup golden raisins
⅓ cup hard cheese, diced
salt, freshly ground pepper
4 tablespoons toasted almonds

Heat the margarine and oil in a pan, and cook the onions and leeks over moderate heat for 3 minutes, stirring occasionally. Add the carrots, zucchini and tomatoes, then stir well, and cook for an additional 1-2 minutes. Stir in the oats. Pour on the stock, stir well and heat to the boiling point. Cover the pan and simmer for 20 minutes. Add the golden raisins and cheese, and season with salt and pepper. Stir with a fork, and cook for an additional 2-3 minutes until the cheese has melted. Scatter with the almonds. Serve hot.

Serve with whole wheat bread and a salad.

CAULIFLOWER AND CHEESE CASSEROLE

1 cauliflower, cut into florets
½ lb calabrese **or** broccoli, cut into florets
salt, freshly ground pepper
1¼ cups lowfat yogurt
2 tablespoons whole wheat flour
1 cup cottage cheese, sieved

a pinch of cayenne pepper
2 tablespoons sunflower margarine, melted
½ cup Edam cheese, grated
1 cup rolled oats
3 tablespoons sunflower seeds

Partially cook the cauliflower and calabrese in boiling salted water for 5-7 minutes until they are barely tender, then drain.

Gradually stir the yogurt into the flour. Heat it over low heat, stirring all the time, until it simmers. Remove from the heat and beat in the cheese. Season with salt, pepper and cayenne pepper.

Arrange the vegetables in a casserole, and pour over the sauce. Mix together the margarine, grated cheese, oats and seeds, and sprinkle this over the sauce. Bake the casserole, uncovered, in a hot oven, 400°F, for 30-35 minutes until bubbling. Serve hot.

Serve with a green or tomato salad.

ABERDEEN PATTIES

MAKES 4

6 oz haddock fillet
1¼ cups skim milk
a few parsley sprigs
1 bay leaf
a sprig of thyme
1 cup rolled oats
½ teaspoon curry powder
salt, freshly ground pepper

2 tablespoons chopped parsley
fine oatmeal for dusting
1 egg, beaten

GARNISH

lemon twists
stuffed olives, sliced

Put the fish into a skillet with the milk, parsley sprigs, bay leaf and thyme. Heat slowly to the boiling point, then simmer for 10 minutes. Lift out the fish, discard any bones and flake it. Strain the milk.

Stir ¾ cup of the oats into the milk. Heat slowly to the boiling point, then simmer for 4 minutes, stirring frequently. Stir in the curry powder, and season with salt and pepper. Remove from the heat and leave to cool. Stir in the flaked fish and the chopped parsley.

Dust your hands with fine oatmeal, and divide the mixture into four pieces. Shape each one into a ball, and press it flat. Dip them in the beaten egg and then in the reserved oats.

Fry the patties in a nonstick pan over moderate heat until golden-brown on each side. Serve hot, garnished with lemon twists and olive slices.

Note Tiny new potatoes and fresh beans are a good accompaniment.

CHICKEN PATTIES

MAKES 4

¾ lb raw chicken, ground
I slice lean bacon, ground
I small onion, finely chopped
8 dried apricots, soaked and drained,
finely chopped
4 tablespoons medium oatmeal
1-2 tablespoons oat bran and
oat germ (optional)
2 tablespoons chopped parsley

salt, freshly ground pepper
I egg, beaten
fine oatmeal for dusting
oil for frying (optional)

GARNISH

onion rings
cucumber slices
lettuce

Mix together the chicken, bacon, onion, apricots, medium oatmeal, oat bran and the parsley. Season with salt and pepper, and bind to a thick paste with the beaten egg.

Dust your hands with fine oatmeal, and divide the mixture into four pieces. Shape each one to form an oval, and press it flat. Dust the patties in oatmeal to cover them.

Brush a skillet with oil, if necessary. Fry the patties over moderate heat for 5 minutes on each side until they are brown. Serve at once, garnished with raw onion rings, cucumber slices and lettuce.

CHICKEN PANCAKES

MAKES 4

I cup whole wheat flour
6 tablespoons rolled oats
salt, freshly ground pepper
2 eggs
1¼ cups skim milk
oil for frying (optional)
6 tablespoons Edam cheese, grated

FILLING

I cup lowfat cream cheese
1¼ cups cooked chicken, diced
2 tablespoons chopped parsley
a pinch of cayenne pepper
a pinch of paprika

Mix together the flour, rolled oats, salt and pepper. Beat in the eggs, and gradually pour on the milk, beating all the time.

Lightly brush an omelet pan with oil, if necessary. Heat the pan over moderate heat, and pour in just enough of the batter to cover the base. Shake the pan, and cook the batter for 2-3 minutes until it bubbles and the underside is brown. Flip or toss the pancake, and cook until the other side is brown. Keep the cooked pancake warm while cooking the remaining batter.

To make the filling, stir together the cream cheese and chicken, stir in the parsley, and season with cayenne pepper and paprika.

Fill the pancakes with the mixture, and roll them up. Arrange them in a single layer in a shallow flameproof dish, and sprinkle the grated cheese on top. Broil the pancakes under moderate heat until the cheese is brown. Serve at once.

Serve with a salad or with grilled tomatoes.

OPPOSITE *Chicken Patties*

Pot Luck

Oats have a long association with warming, welcoming fare, simmering on the stove in the meat, fish or vegetable broth that constitutes the "pot luck" of homely cooking. Scotch broth, at the very heart of Northern tradition, is a fine example, in which rolled oats are cooked with hardy root vegetables in a stock flavored with meat. The dish is not only satisfying, tasty and economical, it also demonstrates one of the principals of healthy cooking – that a little meat can go a long way. We do not have to load our plates with saturated animal fats to enjoy the taste.

In all its various forms, oats are a vegetable soup and stew ingredient, whether using groats to absorb surrounding flavors, or oatmeal and rolled oats to thicken stocks.

Mix rolled oats with flour or bread crumbs to make the kind of dumplings that bob airily to the surface of the broth. Toast oat bread and use it as a garnish or topping – it is especially good spread with crushed garlic. Toast rolled oats with chopped nuts, or mix them with fresh herbs for a quick and easy-sprinkle garnish, or crumble oat cakes to float on top of thick puréed soups.

When it comes to pot luck, oats have a well-deserved air of importance.

CELERIAC SOUP

SERVES 6-8

½ lb celeriac, chopped
2 large carrots, diced
4½ cups chicken stock
1¼ cups skim milk
¼ cup medium oatmeal
salt, freshly ground pepper
½ teaspoon celery seed

2 tablespoons chopped parsley

GARNISH

2 teaspoons celery seed
2 tablespoons jumbo oats, toasted
a few celery leaves

Cook the celeriac and carrots in the stock for 20 minutes until tender, then purée them in a blender. Alternatively, rub them through a sieve, or purée them in a vegetable mill. Return the purée to the pan, and pour on the milk and oatmeal, stirring all the time. Season with salt, pepper and celery seeds, then heat slowly to the boiling point. Just before serving, stir in the chopped parsley. Garnish with the celery seed, oats and a few herb leaves.

CORN CHANDLERS SOUP

1 tablespoon sunflower margarine
1 tablespoon olive oil
1 medium onion, chopped
½ lb carrots, sliced diagonally
2 medium leeks (white part only), sliced
diagonally
2 stalks celery, thinly sliced
¾ cup "soup mix" (dried split peas,
lentils, barley and oatmeal)

¼ cup jumbo oats **or** rolled oats
3¾ cups chicken stock
1 teaspoon mixed dried herbs
1 bouquet garni
salt, freshly ground pepper

GARNISH

grated carrot
watercress sprigs

Heat the margarine and oil in a pan, and fry the onion, carrots, leeks and celery over moderate heat for 2 minutes, stirring all the time. Add the soup mix, oats, stock, herbs and bouquet garni, and stir well. Heat to the boiling point, and boil for 10 minutes, then cover the pan and simmer for 40 minutes. Discard the bouquet garni. Season with salt and pepper, and sprinkle the soup with the grated carrot. Garnish with the watercress. Serve hot.

DUTCH DAIRY SOUP

1 lb potatoes, peeled and cubed
3¾ cups chicken stock
1 tablespoon sunflower margarine
1 large onion, chopped
2 cloves garlic, finely chopped
2 stalks celery, thinly sliced
4 tablespoons coarse oatmeal
1 large carrot, diced
1 small white turnip, diced

½ teaspoon dried thyme
salt, freshly ground pepper
⅔ cup lowfat sour cream
2 tablespoons chopped parsley

GARNISH

8 small slices Oat Bread (page 92)
½ cup Edam cheese, grated
2 tablespoons rolled oats

Cook the potatoes in the stock until tender, then purée them in a blender or press them through a sieve.

Melt the margarine in a pan, and fry the onion, garlic and celery over moderate heat for 3 minutes, stirring frequently. Pour on the potato purée, then add the oatmeal, carrot, turnip and thyme, and stir well. Heat to the boiling point, then cover the pan and simmer for 15-20 minutes until the vegetables are only just tender. Season the soup with salt and pepper, then stir in the sour cream and parsley, and heat slowly.

To make the garnish, toast the bread on both sides. Mix the grated cheese and oats, and spread them on the toast. Place under moderate heat, and broil until the cheese melts.

Float the toasted cheese on the soup, and serve at once.

TWO-MUSHROOM SOUP

¼ lb button mushrooms
1 tablespoon sunflower margarine
1 medium onion, sliced
¼ lb field mushrooms, chopped
3 tablespoons fine oatmeal
2½ cups chicken stock

1¼ cups skim milk
1 tablespoon lemon juice
1 tablespoon mushroom catsup
salt, freshly ground pepper
4 tablespoons lowfat yogurt

Chop half the button mushrooms and slice the remainder. Melt the margarine in a pan, and fry the onion and chopped button and field mushrooms over low heat for 7-8 minutes, stirring frequently. Stir in the oatmeal, and cook for 1 minute. Slowly pour on the stock and the milk, stirring all the time. Stir in the lemon juice and mushroom catsup, and season with salt and pepper. Heat slowly to the boiling point, then cover and simmer for 10 minutes. Swirl the yogurt on top of the soup just before serving, then add the sliced mushrooms. Serve hot.

Variation
For a smooth soup, purée the vegetables and liquid in a blender, or press the vegetables through a sieve. Return the purée to the pan, and reheat gently.

NORTHERN GAZPACHO

1¼ cups tomato juice
1 tablespoon concentrated
tomato paste
2 tablespoons cider vinegar
⅔ cup chicken stock
1 teaspoon Worcestershire
sauce
2 tomatoes, skinned and sliced
salt, freshly ground pepper
1 small onion, finely chopped

1 leek (white part only), finely chopped
¼ cucumber, finely diced
1 red pepper, seeded and chopped
4 tablespoons jumbo oats
2 tablespoons chopped parsley
1 tablespoon snipped chives

GARNISH

2 Oat cakes (page 20), crumbled

Purée the tomato juice, tomato paste, vinegar, stock, sauce and tomatoes in a blender. Alternatively, rub the tomatoes through a sieve, and mix them with the liquid ingredients. Season the soup with salt and pepper. Stir in the prepared vegetables and the oats, then cover and chill for at least 1 hour.

Just before serving, stir in the herbs, and sprinkle with the oat cake crumbs. Serve in chilled bowls.

OPPOSITE *Lemon Soup, Lamb Broth with Oat Dumplings (page 40) and Northern Gazpacho*

LEMON SOUP

½ cup yellow split peas, soaked and
drained
2½ cups medium oatmeal
1 tablespoon oat bran and
oat germ (optional)
1 medium onion, finely chopped
2 stalks celery, thinly sliced
grated rind of 1 lemon

juice of 1½ lemons
½ teaspoon turmeric
4½ cups chicken stock (approx)
salt, freshly ground pepper

GARNISH

scallions, sliced
lemon slices

Put the split peas, oatmeal, oat bran, onion, celery, lemon rind and juice, turmeric and
stock into a pan, and heat to the boiling point. Cover the pan, and simmer for 1 hour,
adjusting the liquid as necessary. Season with salt and pepper. Stir the soup well, and
sprinkle with the sliced scallions. Float the lemon slices on top. Serve hot.

SCOTS OATMEAL SOUP

SERVES 4-6

1 tablespoon sunflower margarine
1 large onion, finely chopped
4 tablespoons medium oatmeal
2½ cups chicken stock
a few parsley sprigs
1¼ cups buttermilk

salt, freshly ground pepper
2 egg yolks, beaten

GARNISH

2 tablespoons chopped parsley

Melt the margarine in a pan, and cook the onion over moderate heat for 3 minutes, stirring once or twice. Stir in the oatmeal, and cook for 1 minute. Slowly pour on the stock, stirring all the time, then add the parsley sprigs. Heat to the boiling point, then cover the pan and simmer for 30 minutes. Discard the parsley.

Purée the soup in a blender, or rub the mixture through a sieve. Return the purée to the pan, slowly pour on the buttermilk, and heat slowly to the boiling point. Season with salt and pepper. Pour a little of the soup onto the egg yolks, then pour them into the soup, and heat over low heat. Serve hot, garnished with the parsley.

MEDITERRANEAN CHOWDER

2 tablespoons olive oil
1 large onion, thinly sliced
4 stalks celery, thinly sliced
2 cloves garlic, finely chopped
1 lb tomatoes, skinned
2 bay leaves
1½ cups potatoes, peeled and diced
2½ cups fish **or** vegetable stock
2 tablespoons concentrated
tomato paste

1½ lb white fish fillets cut into 1½ inch
squares
2 tablespoons chopped parsley
¼ lb shelled cooked shrimp
salt, freshly ground pepper
4 cloves garlic, crushed
4 slices Oat Bread (page 92)
1 small leek (white part only) thinly sliced
into rings

Heat the oil in a pan, and fry the onion, celery and garlic over moderate heat for 3 minutes, stirring occasionally. Add the tomatoes, bay leaves, potatoes, stock and tomato paste, and stir well. Heat to the boiling point, then cover and simmer for 10 minutes. Add the fish and chopped parsley, then heat to the boiling point. Cover and simmer for 10 minutes, then add the prawns, and season with salt and pepper. Cover and simmer for an additional 5 minutes.

Rub the crushed garlic into the bread slices, then cut the bread into small squares. Place in the bottom of a heated serving dish, and pour on the chowder. Scatter the leeks on top.

COCK-A-LEEKIE

SERVES 6

3 lb chicken, including giblets
1 bouquet garni
8 medium leeks, cut into 1 inch slices
½ cup jumbo oats

12 prunes, soaked, drained and pitted
salt, freshly ground pepper

GARNISH

chopped parsley

Skin the chicken, then put it into a pan with the giblets, bouquet garni and half the leeks. Cover with water, and heat slowly to the boiling point. Skim off any fat and foam that rises to the surface. Cover the pan and simmer for 1½ hours.

Remove the chicken from the stock, and leave to cool, then cut the meat from the bones, and cut it into chunks.

Strain the stock and discard the vegetables and giblets. Measure 5 cups of stock and return it to the pan, then add the remaining leeks, the oats and prunes. Cover the pan and simmer for 15 minutes. Add the chicken, then season with salt and pepper, and heat gently. Serve hot, garnished with the parsley.

Oat Cakes (see page 20) are a good accompaniment.

SCOTCH BROTH

SERVES 6-8

1 lb stewing beef, chopped
7½ cups water
1¾ cups rutabagas, diced
2 medium carrots, thinly sliced
1 large onion, chopped
1 leek (white part only), thinly sliced
1 bay leaf
1½ cups white cabbage, shredded

6 tablespoons rolled oats
1 tablespoon concentrated
tomato paste
salt, freshly ground pepper
2 tablespoons chopped parsley

GARNISH

1 dessert apple, cored and thinly sliced

Fry the beef in a nonstick pan over moderate heat, stirring frequently, until the fat runs. Lift out the meat with a slotted spoon, and discard the fat. Return the meat to the pan. Pour on the water, and heat to the boiling point. Skim off any fat and foam that rises to the surface. Cover the pan and simmer for 1 hour, then skim again. Add the rutabagas, carrots, onion, leek and bay leaf, and heat to the boiling point. Cover the pan and simmer for an additional hour. Add the cabbage, then stir in the tomato paste. Add the oats, and season with salt and pepper. Heat to the boiling point, then cover the pan and simmer for 10 minutes. Discard the bay leaf, and season to taste, then stir in the parsley. Garnish the soup – in an un-Scots way! – with the apple slices. Serve hot.

GOULASH SOUP

SERVES 6

¾ lb lean beef, ground
1 large onion, chopped
3 tablespoons medium oatmeal
1 tablespoon paprika
½ teaspoon caraway seeds
1 clove garlic, crushed
14 oz canned tomatoes
2½ cups beef stock

1 tablespoon concentrated
tomato paste
1 red pepper, seeded and chopped
3 tablespoons jumbo oats
1½ cups potatoes, peeled and cubed
salt, freshly ground pepper
⅔ cup lowfat yogurt
2 tablespoons chopped parsley

Fry the beef in a nonstick pan over moderate heat, stirring all the time, until the fat runs. Lift out the meat with a slotted spoon, and discard the fat. Return the meat to the pan, then stir in the onion, oatmeal, paprika, caraway seeds and garlic, and cook for 2 minutes, stirring frequently. Add the tomatoes and their juice, and the stock, and heat slowly to the boiling point. Cover the pan and simmer for 30 minutes. Stir in the tomato paste, red pepper, oats and potatoes, and season with salt and pepper. Cover the pan and cook for an additional 15 minutes. Season to taste. Skim off any fat from the top of the soup. Swirl the yogurt over the top of the soup just before serving, and sprinkle with the parsley.

CHILI POT

⅔ cup dried red kidney beans, soaked
and drained (see **Note**)
¾ cup oat groats, soaked and drained
½ lb lean beef, ground
2 tablespoons sunflower oil
2 medium onions, sliced
2 green peppers, seeded and sliced
2 red peppers, seeded and sliced
4 stalks celery, thinly sliced
2 red chili peppers, seeded and
chopped

2 tablespoons medium oatmeal
1 tablespoon oat bran and
oat germ (optional)
1 tablespoon paprika
½ teaspoon cayenne pepper
1¼ cups beef stock
2 medium carrots, diced
salt, freshly ground pepper
2 tablespoons chopped cilantro **or**
parsley

Boil the kidney beans briskly in fresh water for at least 10 minutes, then cook for 50 minutes. Meanwhile, cook the groats in a separate pan of boiling water for 1 hour. Drain the beans and groats.

Fry the beef in a nonstick pan over moderate heat, stirring all the time, until the fat runs. Remove the meat with a slotted spoon, and discard the fat.

Heat the oil in a flameproof casserole, and fry the onions, peppers, celery and chili peppers over moderate heat for 4 minutes, stirring frequently. Add the meat, oatmeal, oat bran, paprika and cayenne pepper, stir well and cook for 1 minute. Pour on the stock, then add the beans, groats and carrots. Heat to the boiling point, stir well, then cover the pan. Simmer for 45 minutes, then season with salt and pepper, and stir in the herbs. Serve hot.

Note It is important to discard the draining water used for soaking the kidney beans.

OPPOSITE *Chili Pot*

LAMB BROTH WITH OAT DUMPLINGS

1½ lb lamb shanks
6 cups water
1⅛ cups oat groats, soaked and drained
4 leeks (white part only), sliced
8 small carrots, cut into chunks
4 stalks celery, cut into chunks
1 small turnip, diced
salt, freshly ground pepper
2 tablespoons chopped parsley

DUMPLINGS

½ cup whole wheat flour
3½ tablespoons oat bran and
oat germ
salt, freshly ground pepper
2 tablespoons sunflower margarine
2-3 tablespoons water
2 tablespoons rolled oats

Put the lamb, water and groats in a pan. Heat slowly to the boiling point, then skim off any fat and foam that rises to the top. Cover and simmer for 1½ hours, then skim again. Add the vegetables, and season with salt and pepper, then cover and simmer for an additional hour.

Lift out the meat and bones with a slotted spoon. Discard the bones. Return the meat to the pan, and leave overnight if possible. Lift off any fat that has settled on top of the pan.

To make the dumplings, mix together the flour, oat bran and oat germ, salt and pepper, then rub in the margarine. Sprinkle on enough water to make a firm dough. Shape the dough into small balls, then roll them in the oats.

Reheat the broth until boiling, and season to taste. Add the dumplings, and simmer for 10 minutes, then stir in the chopped parsley. Serve at once.

LAMB REVITHIA

⅔ cup dried chickpeas, soaked and
drained
¾ cup oat groats, soaked and drained
¾ lb lean leg of lamb, cubed
2 tablespoons olive oil
1 medium onion, sliced
1 clove garlic, finely chopped
1 teaspoon paprika
¼ teaspoon grated nutmeg

1 tablespoon fine oatmeal
1 tablespoon concentrated
tomato paste
2 cups hot chicken stock
1 tablespoon lemon juice
2 tablespoons chopped parsley
salt, freshly ground pepper
4 tablespoons lowfat yogurt
1 tablespoon chopped cilantro **or** parsley

Cook the chickpeas and the groats in separate pans of boiling water for 1 hour, then drain.

Fry the cubes of meat in a nonstick pan over moderate heat until browned, turning them often. Remove the meat with a slotted spoon, and discard the fat.

Heat the oil in a flameproof casserole, and cook the onion and garlic over moderate heat for 3 minutes, stirring once or twice. Stir in the paprika and nutmeg, and cook for 1 minute. Stir in the oatmeal and tomato paste, and cook for an additional minute. Add the meat, then pour on the hot stock and lemon juice, stirring all the time. Heat to boiling point, then cover and simmer over low heat for 1 hour. Add the chickpeas and groats, then heat to the boiling point. Cover, then simmer for an additional hour. Stir in the chopped parsley, and season with salt and pepper. Swirl the yogurt over the casserole just before serving, and sprinkle with the chopped herbs. Serve hot.

POACHER'S STEW

2½ tablespoons fine oatmeal
salt, freshly ground pepper
2 teaspoons dried basil
½ teaspoon ground mace
2 lb rabbit portions
3 tablespoons sunflower margarine
3 medium onions, thinly sliced
2 cloves garlic, finely chopped
5 medium carrots, diced
2 stalks celery, thinly sliced
2 tablespoons concentrated
tomato paste

2½ cups hot chicken stock
2 tomatoes, skinned and sliced
1 tablespoon lemon juice
2 tablespoons jumbo oats **or** rolled oats
2 tablespoons chopped parsley

GARNISH

4 slices Oat Bread (page 92), cut into
triangles, toasted

Put the oatmeal, salt, pepper, basil and mace into a bag, then toss the rabbit portions in the mixture to coat them thoroughly.

Melt the margarine in a flameproof casserole, and fry the rabbit portions over moderate heat, turning them to brown them evenly on all sides. Remove with a slotted spoon, and keep warm.

Put the onions, garlic, carrots and celery in the casserole, stir well and fry for 3 minutes, stirring occasionally. Stir in any remaining oatmeal.

Stir the tomato paste into the hot stock, then pour it slowly onto the vegetables, stirring all the time. Add the tomatoes, and heat to the boiling point. Return the rabbit to the casserole, and heat again to the boiling point, then cover and simmer for 1½ hours or until the rabbit is tender. Remove the rabbit with a slotted spoon, and keep warm.

Purée the vegetables and stock in a blender, then sieve the purée. Alternatively, rub the vegetables through a sieve or purée them in a vegetable mill. Stir the lemon juice and oats into the purée, then season to taste. Return the purée to the casserole, add the rabbit, and reheat gently, stirring in the parsley. Garnish with the triangles of toast.

CRUNCHY SPICED VEGETABLES

SERVES 4-6

2 tablespoons sunflower margarine
1 tablespoon sunflower oil
2 medium onions, sliced
2 cloves garlic, finely chopped
1 piece of fresh ginger root, peeled and
finely chopped
1 teaspoon ground coriander
1 teaspoon curry powder
½ teaspoon coriander seeds,
lightly crushed
½ teaspoon cardamom pods,
lightly crushed
1 medium cauliflower, cut into florets
3 medium carrots, thinly sliced
2 medium zucchini, sliced

1 green pepper, seeded and sliced
1 red pepper, seeded and sliced
½ lb green beans
1 dessert apple, cored and sliced
1¼ cups chicken stock
4 tablespoons coarse oatmeal
salt, freshly ground pepper

GARNISH

4 tablespoons jumbo oats, toasted
3 tablespoons chopped
almonds, toasted
1 tablespoon sunflower
seeds, toasted

Heat the margarine and oil in a flameproof casserole, and cook the onions, garlic and ginger over moderate heat for 3 minutes, stirring frequently. Stir in the spices, and cook for 1 minute. Add the vegetables, apple, stock and oatmeal, stir well and heat slowly to the boiling point. Cover the pan and simmer for 20 minutes, stirring occasionally, until the vegetables are just tender. Season with salt and pepper. Sprinkle the oats, almonds and seeds over the vegetables, and serve hot.

Serve with cooked oat groats.

OPPOSITE *Vegetable Basket*

VEGETABLE BASKET

2 tablespoons sunflower oil
1 medium onion, sliced
4 stalks celery, thinly sliced
2 medium carrots, thinly sliced
½ small white cabbage, shredded
2 medium zucchini, sliced
½ teaspoon cumin seeds
1 tablespoon paprika
1 teaspoon dried oregano

1 tablespoon concentrated
tomato paste
2½ cups tomato juice
1¼ cups chicken stock
salt, freshly ground pepper
4 tablespoons jumbo oats **or**
rolled oats
⅔ cup lowfat sour cream
chopped marjoram **or** parsley

Heat the oil in a flameproof casserole, and fry the onion and celery over moderate heat for 3 minutes, stirring once or twice. Add the carrots, cabbage and zucchinis, and cook for 5 minutes, stirring frequently. Stir in the cumin seeds, paprika and dried oregano, and cook for 1 minute, then add the tomato paste, tomato juice and stock. Stir well and heat to the boiling point. Cover the pan and simmer for 15 minutes or until the vegetables are just tender. Season with salt and pepper, then stir in the oats and all but 2 tablespoons of the sour cream. Heat gently. Swirl the remaining sour cream over the vegetables, and scatter the top with the fresh herbs. Serve hot.
    Serve this vegetable hotpot sprinkled with uncooked oat groats.

The Main Attraction

When you have added oats and oatmeal to pastry and pizza dough and to a savory filling for poultry, fish and vegetables; tossed whole fish and fillets of meat in an oat crumb mixture; made a colorful and tasty pilaf with oat groats; finished off a hearty casserole with a cheesy oat topping; and extended the meat content in pies, loaves and fillings with this fiber-full cereal, you will wonder what, if anything, oats cannot do.

Fine oatmeal stirred into a sauce is a soluble fiber thickening agent; medium or coarse grades – steel-cut oatmeal – and rolled oats can be used in place of bread crumbs to provide the "bulk" in fillings; and used to extend meat they both absorb the flavor and enable you to cut down on saturated animal fat. As broiled or baked toppings, rolled oats need to be mixed with a moist vegetable – tomatoes for example – fat or cheese if they are not to burn. A Dutch hard cheese which is lowest in fat content or, better still, cottage cheese is suitable.

"If you use oats in all these ways, doesn't everything begin to taste like porridge?" a colleague asked doubtfully. Well, there's only one way to find out. Here's another chapter of recipes – the proof of the pudding.

NORWICH BAKED VEGETABLES

1 small cauliflower, cut into florets
2 medium carrots, diced
1 medium parsnip, diced
salt, freshly ground pepper
½ cup cooked dried navy beans

SAUCE

2 tablespoons sunflower margarine
2 tablespoons oat bran and
oat germ

1 teaspoon dry English mustard
1¼ cups buttermilk
½ cup cottage cheese
2 tablespoons chopped parsley

TOPPING

½ cup rolled oats
½ cup chopped hazelnuts
½ cup cottage cheese

Steam the cauliflower, carrots and parsnip over boiling salted water until tender. Transfer them to a baking dish, then stir in the navy beans.

To make the sauce, melt the margarine in a small pan, and stir in the oat bran and mustard until the mixture is smooth. Slowly pour on the buttermilk, stirring constantly. Heat the sauce to the boiling point, and simmer for 3 minutes. Season with salt and pepper. Stir in the cottage cheese and the parsley, then pour the sauce over the vegetables.

Mix together the topping ingredients, and sprinkle them over the vegetables. Bake in a moderately hot oven, 375°F, for 35 minutes until the topping is brown and crisp.

VEGETABLE DECKER

2 tablespoons sunflower oil
1 large onion, sliced
2 zucchini, diced
1 eggplant, diced
4 stalks celery, thinly sliced
2 red peppers, seeded and chopped
1½ cups mushrooms, sliced
3 tomatoes, skinned and sliced
1 cup chicken stock

1 teaspoon dried mixed herbs
salt, freshly ground pepper
¼ cup rolled oats

FILLING

1 cup whole wheat bread crumbs
½ cup rolled oats
¼ cup jumbo oats
½ cup Edam cheese, grated

Heat the oil in a skillet, and fry all the vegetables over moderate heat for 2-3 minutes, stirring frequently. Pour on the stock, add the herbs, and season with salt and pepper. Heat to the boiling point, then simmer, uncovered, for 5 minutes. Stir in the oats.

Mix together the filling ingredients, and layer alternately in a baking dish with the vegetables. Cover with foil or a lid, and bake in a moderately hot oven, 375°F, for 30 minutes. Remove the lid, and bake for an additional 10 minutes to brown the topping.

SARDINE PIZZA

1½ cups whole wheat self-rising flour
½ cup rolled oats
salt, freshly ground pepper
4 tablespoons sunflower margarine
1 teaspoon dried mixed herbs
6 tablespoons lowfat yogurt
fine oatmeal for dusting

FILLING AND TOPPING

14 oz canned tomatoes
1 small onion, sliced
1 clove garlic, crushed
1 teaspoon dried mixed herbs
1 medium zucchini, diced
2 tablespoons fine oatmeal
salt, freshly ground pepper
8 oz sardines in oil, drained
2 tablespoons black olives,
halved and pitted
4 thin slices Gruyère **or** Edam cheese

Make the filling first. Put the tomatoes, onion, garlic, herbs and zucchini into a small pan. Heat to the boiling point, then simmer for 20 minutes. Sprinkle on the oatmeal, and quickly stir it in. Season with salt and pepper. Simmer again if necessary to reduce to a thick paste. Set aside to cool.

Meanwhile, mix together the flour and oats, and season with salt and pepper. Rub in the margarine. Stir in the herbs, and mix to a firm dough with the yogurt. Lightly dust a sheet of parchment paper with fine oatmeal. Roll out the dough and shape it to an 8 inch circle, pressing up the edges.

Place the dough on a baking sheet. Spread it with the cooled tomato filling. Split the sardines in half lengthwise, and remove the bones. Arrange them, cut sides down, in a wheel pattern. Arrange the olives, and cover the sardines with the cheese. Bake in a hot oven, 425°F, for 15-20 minutes until crisp. Serve hot.

MUSHROOM QUICHE

2 tablespoons sunflower margarine
1 small onion, finely chopped
1 clove garlic, crushed
½ lb button mushrooms, sliced
½ cup cottage cheese, sieved
⅔ cup lowfat sour cream
⅔ cup skim milk
1 tablespoon chopped parsley
2 eggs

salt, freshly ground pepper

RICH OATMEAL PASTRY

¾ cup rolled oats
¾ cup whole wheat self-rising flour
salt
6 tablespoons sunflower margarine
1 egg, beaten
fine oatmeal for dusting

Make the pastry first. Mix together the oats, flour and salt. Rub in the margarine, and bind the mixture to a dough with the beaten egg. Lightly dust a sheet of parchment paper with fine oatmeal. Roll out the dough to ¼ inch thickness, and use to line an 8 inch quiche ring. Trim the edges, and prick the base with a fork.

Melt the margarine in a pan, and fry the onion and garlic over moderate heat for 3 minutes, stirring once or twice. Cool slightly.

Spread the onion and garlic over the quiche shell, and arrange the mushrooms on top. Beat together the cheese, sour cream, milk, parsley and eggs, and season with salt and pepper. Pour the filling over the mushrooms. Stand the quiche on a baking sheet, and bake in a moderately hot oven, 375°F, for 35 minutes until the filling is set. Serve hot.

GARDEN VEGETABLE TART

½ lb small green beans
1½ lbs broad beans fava, shelled
2 medium carrots, thinly sliced
2 medium zucchini, thinly sliced
⅔ cup canned corn kernels, drained
salt, freshly ground pepper
1¼ cups buttermilk
2 teaspoons lemon juice
2 tablespoons chopped parsley

2 eggs

OATMEAL PASTRY

⅓ cup medium oatmeal
¼ cup jumbo oats
¾ cup whole wheat flour
salt
6 tablespoons sunflower margarine
fine oatmeal for dusting

Steam the vegetables over boiling salted water until just tender. Plunge them into cold water to prevent further cooking, then drain. Set aside to cool.

Meanwhile, make the pastry. Mix together the oatmeal, oats, flour and salt. Rub in the margarine, and sprinkle on enough water to make a firm dough. Lightly dust a sheet of parchment paper with fine oatmeal. Roll out the dough to ¼ inch thickness, and use to line an 8 inch quiche ring. Trim the edges, and prick the base with a fork.

Beat together the buttermilk, lemon juice, parsley and eggs, and season to taste.

Spread the cooled vegetables in the quiche shell. Pour on the buttermilk mixture, then stand the tart on a baking sheet. Bake in a moderately hot oven, 375°F, for 35 minutes or until the filling is set. Serve warm.

OPPOSITE *Mushroom Quiche, Sardine Pizza (page 45)* and *Garden Vegetable Tart*

CARROT CRUMBLE

1 lb cooked carrots, thinly sliced
1 tablespoon sunflower margarine
½ teaspoon ground ginger
1 teaspoon clear honey
1⅓ cups canned corn kernels, drained
1 tablespoon chopped parsley
⅓ cup chicken stock
salt, freshly ground pepper

TOPPING

⅓ cup medium oatmeal
2 tablespoons sesame seeds
2 tablespoons chopped hazelnuts
salt, freshly ground pepper
4 tablespoons sunflower oil

Mix the carrots with the margarine, ginger, honey, corn, parsley and chicken stock, then season with salt and pepper. Pour the vegetable mixture into a baking dish.

Mix together the topping ingredients, and spread this over the vegetables. Bake in a moderately hot oven, 375°F, for 20 minutes until the topping is crisp and brown. Serve hot.

Note A green salad is a specially good contrast and complement to this dish.

CABBAGE ROLLS

12 large, tender cabbage leaves, stalks removed
salt, freshly ground pepper
1 tablespoon concentrated tomato paste
1¼ cups hot chicken stock

FILLING

2 tablespoons sunflower margarine
1 tablespoon sunflower oil
1 medium onion, chopped

2 stalks tender celery, finely chopped
1½ cups chopped hazelnuts
½ cup rolled oats
⅓ cup dried apricots, chopped, soaked and drained
3 tablespoons chopped parsley
1 teaspoon dried oregano
salt, freshly ground pepper
a pinch of grated nutmeg
2 eggs, beaten

Cook the cabbage leaves in boiling salted water for 3 minutes, then drain and pat dry with paper towels.

To make the filling, heat the margarine and oil in a pan, and fry the onion and celery over moderate heat for 3 minutes, stirring once or twice. Stir in the nuts and oats, and remove from the heat. Stir in the apricots and herbs, and season the mixture with salt, pepper and nutmeg. Beat in the eggs.

Place the cabbage leaves flat, with the stalk side towards you. Place a spoonful of the mixture in the center of each leaf. Fold over the stalk end, then each of the two sides to enclose the filling. Make neat packages and place them, seam side down, in a skillet.

Mix the tomato paste with the hot stock, and season with salt and pepper. Pour it over the leaves, cover the pan, heat to the boiling point, then simmer for 30 minutes. Serve hot.

Note Potatoes steamed in their skins go well with this dish.

ZUCCHINI CRISP

2 tablespoons sunflower oil
1 lb zucchini, cut into
¼ inch slices
1 small eggplant, thinly sliced
2 cloves garlic, crushed
2 tomatoes, skinned and sliced
1 teaspoon dried marjoram
2 tablespoons chopped parsley
salt, freshly ground pepper

SAUCE AND TOPPING

1 cup cottage cheese, sieved
2 eggs
1 ¼ cups lowfat yogurt
salt, freshly ground pepper
a pinch of grated nutmeg
½ cup chopped walnuts
½ cup jumbo oats

Heat a little of the oil in a skillet, and fry the zucchini and eggplant slices in batches to brown them lightly, greasing the pan with a little more oil each time.

Transfer the vegetables to a baking dish. Fry the garlic over moderate heat for 1 minute. Add the tomato slices and herbs, and cook for 2-3 minutes. Spread the tomatoes over the dish, and season with salt and pepper.

To make the sauce, beat together half the cheese, the eggs and yogurt, and season with salt, pepper and nutmeg. Pour the sauce over the dish.

Mix the walnuts and oats with the remaining cheese, and sprinkle this over the sauce. Stand the dish on a baking sheet, and bake in a moderately hot oven, 375°F, for 30-35 minutes until the topping is crisp and brown. Serve hot.

BEAN PEPPERS

4 large green **or** red peppers
⅔ cup chicken stock

FILLING

1 scant cup cooked dried beans, e.g., navy
or flageolet
1 small onion, finely chopped
2 cloves garlic, crushed
½ cup rolled oats

½ cup chopped walnuts
¾ cup mushrooms, chopped
2 large tomatoes, skinned and chopped
salt, freshly ground pepper
1 teaspoon dried savory
1 tablespoon chopped parsley
2 tablespoons sunflower
margarine, melted
4 tablespoons cottage cheese

Cut a thin slice from the top of each of the peppers. Remove the seeds and core. Blanch the peppers and tops in boiling water for 5 minutes. Drain them and stand the peppers upside down to dry.

To make the filling, mix together the beans, onion, garlic, oats, walnuts, mushrooms and tomatoes. Season the mixture with salt, pepper and the herbs, then pour on the margarine, and mix well.

Stand the peppers upright in a greased baking dish that just fits them. Pack the filling into the peppers, mounding it into a dome on top. Press the cottage cheese onto the filling. Pour the stock around the peppers, then bake in a moderate oven, 350°F, for 30 minutes until the filling is bubbling. Serve hot.

SPICED LENTIL PILAF

2 tablespoons sunflower oil
2 medium onions, chopped
2 cloves garlic, finely chopped
1 green pepper, seeded and chopped
1 red pepper, seeded and chopped
1 teaspoon ground cumin
1 teaspoon curry powder
½ teaspoon turmeric
1 scant cup oat groats, soaked and
drained
½ cup rolled oats
4 cups chicken stock (approx)
1⅛ cups brown lentils, washed and
drained
4 tablespoons seedless raisins
4 tablespoons cashew nuts

2 tablespoons chopped cilantro
or parsley
salt, freshly ground pepper

SAUCE

⅔ cup lowfat yogurt
2 tablespoons chopped cilantro
or parsley
1 teaspoon lemon juice
paprika

GARNISH

banana slices
lemon juice
3 tablespoons flaked coconut

Heat the oil in a flameproof casserole, and fry the onions and garlic over moderate heat for 2 minutes. Stir in the green and red peppers, and cook for an additional 2 minutes. Stir in the spices, groats and rolled oats, and cook for 1 minute. Pour on the stock. Heat to the boiling point, then simmer for 30 minutes. Add the lentils. Heat to the boiling point, then simmer for 45 minutes. Add more stock or water if the dish begins to dry out. Stir in the raisins, nuts and herbs, and season with salt and pepper. Simmer for 2-3 minutes.

Meanwhile, stir together the yogurt, cilantro and lemon juice for the sauce. Sprinkle with the paprika.

Garnish the pilaf with the banana slices tossed in lemon juice, and sprinkle the coconut on top. Serve the sauce separately.

NUT PILAF

1⅛ cups oat groats, soaked and drained
2 tablespoons sunflower oil
1 medium onion, thinly sliced
1 clove garlic, crushed
4 stalks celery, thinly sliced
1 red pepper, seeded and chopped

1 green pepper, seeded and chopped
¾ cup walnuts, chopped
½ lb button mushrooms, sliced
4 tablespoons white wine
salt, freshly ground pepper
2 teaspoons chopped thyme

Cook the groats in boiling water for 1¼ hours, then drain thoroughly and rinse under cold, running water.

Heat the oil in a pan, and cook the onion and garlic over moderate heat for 3 minutes, stirring once or twice. Add the celery, red and green peppers, the nuts, mushrooms and groats. Stir well, then cook for 2 minutes, stirring frequently. Pour on the wine, and season with salt and pepper. Simmer for 5 minutes, then stir in the thyme. Serve hot.

Serve with a green salad.

Spiced Lentil Pilaf

GINGER AND PEANUT LOAF

2 tablespoons sunflower oil
1 large onion, chopped
1 clove garlic, finely chopped
1 red pepper, seeded and chopped
1 piece ginger root, peeled, chopped
and crushed
1½ cups mushrooms, chopped
2½ tablespoons fine oatmeal
1½ cups unsalted peanuts, ground
4 tomatoes, skinned and chopped

1 tablespoon concentrated
tomato paste
¾ cup rolled oats
1 tablespoon clear honey
1 tablespoon soy sauce
3 tablespoons medium sherry
2 tablespoons orange juice
1 teaspoon grated orange rind
1 egg, beaten
6-8 young spinach leaves, without stalks
(optional)

Heat the oil in a pan, and fry the onion, garlic, pepper and ginger over moderate heat for 3 minutes, stirring frequently. Stir in the mushrooms, and cook over low heat for 5 minutes. Stir in the oatmeal, and cook for 1 minute. Remove the pan from the heat, then stir in the peanuts, tomato paste, tomatoes and oats. Mix together the honey, soy sauce, sherry, orange juice and rind and the egg. Pour this onto the nut mixture, and beat until smooth.

Line a greased 1 lb loaf pan with the spinach leaves, if used. Fill the pan with the nut mixture, and cover with foil. Stand the pan in a roasting pan half-filled with warm water, and bake in a moderately hot oven, 375°F, for 50 minutes. Leave in the pan for 5 minutes, then turn out. Serve hot, with vegetables, or cold, with salad.

SEAFOOD ZUCCHINI

½ lb fillet of cod **or** haddock
1 scant cup skim milk
1 medium onion, halved
1 clove
1 bay leaf
4 tablespoons rolled oats
2 tablespoons jumbo oats

4 large zucchini
1 tablespoon sunflower oil
⅔ cup cottage cheese
1 egg
salt, freshly ground pepper
2 tablespoons chopped parsley
½ cup Edam cheese, grated

Poach the fish for 10 minutes in the milk with half the onion, the clove and bay leaf. Lift out the fish. Remove any bones, and flake the fish. Discard the onion, clove and bay leaf. Stir the oats into the milk, and heat to the boiling point, stirring constantly. Remove from the heat.

Trim and halve the zucchini and scoop out the flesh, taking care not to pierce the skins. Chop the flesh.

Chop the remaining onion half. Heat the oil in a pan, and fry the onion and zucchini flesh over moderate heat for 3 minutes, stirring frequently.

Beat the zucchini mixture, the flaked fish, cottage cheese and egg into the oats, then season with salt and pepper, and stir in the parsley.

Place the zucchini halves in a shallow baking dish. Pack the mixture into the shells, and shape into neat mounds. Sprinkle with the grated cheese. Bake in a hot oven, 400°F, for 30 minutes until bubbling. Serve hot.

Note New potatoes and a green vegetable such as calabrese complete a light meal. Alternatively, you can serve the zucchini with a green salad and tomatoes.

HOT PEPPER FISH

4 haddock fillets (approximately 1½ lb)
14 oz canned tomatoes
1 red pepper, seeded and sliced
1 green pepper, seeded and sliced
1 large onion, thinly sliced
1 teaspoon dried tarragon
½ teaspoon Tabasco sauce
salt, freshly ground pepper

TOPPING

½ cup rolled oats
½ cup whole wheat flour
salt, freshly ground pepper
½ cup cottage cheese
¼ cup Gruyère **or** Edam cheese, grated

Place the fish in a greased baking dish.

Put the canned tomatoes into a pan, and add the sliced peppers, onion, tarragon and Tabasco sauce. Season with salt and pepper. Heat to the boiling point, then simmer for 15 minutes until the mixture thickens. Remove from the heat.

Mix together the ingredients for the topping.

Pour the tomato sauce over the fish, and spread the topping evenly over it. Place the dish on a baking sheet, and bake in a moderately hot oven, 375°F, for 15 minutes until bubbling.

SPECKLED TROUT

4 trout, scaled, cleaned, washed and dried
3 tablespoons fine oatmeal
1 teaspoon dried thyme
2 tablespoons sunflower margarine

FILLING AND COATING

2 tablespoons sunflower margarine
1 small onion, finely chopped
2 slices bacon, chopped
2 tablespoons medium oatmeal

⅔ cup canned corn kernels, drained
2 tablespoons chopped parsley
2 tablespoons lemon juice
2 teaspoons grated lemon rind
salt, freshly ground pepper

GARNISH

lemon wedges

Prepare the filling first. Melt the margarine in a pan, and fry the onion and bacon over moderate heat for 3 minutes, stirring once or twice. Stir in the medium oatmeal, corn, parsley, lemon juice and half the lemon rind. Season with salt and pepper, then remove from the heat. Leave to cool.

Pack the filling into the fish cavities. Mix the remaining lemon rind with the fine oatmeal and dried thyme. Toss the fish in this mixture to coat it thoroughly on all sides.

Line a broiler pan with foil. Melt the remaining margarine in a pan. Brush the foil with the margarine, and place the fish on it side by side. Drizzle the rest of the margarine over the fish. Broil under moderate heat for 5-6 minutes on each side. Serve at once, garnished with the lemon wedges.

Note Tomato salad garnished with thinly sliced onion rings is a good accompaniment.

COD STEAKS WITH OLIVES

4 cod steaks (approximately 1½ lb), boned
½ cup Edam cheese, grated

FILLING

2 tablespoons sunflower margarine
1 small onion, chopped
½ green pepper, seeded and chopped
2 tablespoons medium oatmeal

1 tablespoon jumbo oats
1 tablespoon chopped parsley
1 teaspoon grated orange rind
2 tablespoons orange juice
3 tablespoons black olives, pitted and chopped
freshly ground pepper

Make the filling first. Melt the margarine in a pan, and fry the onion and pepper over moderate heat for 3 minutes, stirring frequently. Remove from the heat and stir in the oatmeal, oats, parsley, orange rind, orange juice and olives. Season with pepper.

Place the cod steaks in a greased shallow baking dish. Pack the filling into the bone cavity, and sprinkle with the cheese. Bake in a moderate oven, 350°F, for 20 minutes until bubbling. Serve hot.

Note New potatoes, and corn tossed in yogurt and chopped parsley complete a nutritious meal.

OPPOSITE *Hake Stir-fry*

HAKE STIR-FRY

1 ½ lb hake, skinned, filleted and cut into 1 inch slices
4 tablespoons orange juice
1 teaspoon grated orange rind
3 tablespoons fine oatmeal
salt, freshly ground pepper
a pinch of ground mace
1 teaspoon fennel seed
2 tablespoons sunflower oil

1 medium onion, sliced
1 clove garlic, finely chopped
1 red pepper, seeded and sliced
1 green pepper, seeded and sliced
3 stalks celery, thinly sliced
4 tablespoons cashew nuts
2 tablespoons jumbo oats
1 tablespoon chopped parsley
strips of orange rind

Toss the fish in the orange juice and orange rind. Cover and leave to marinate for at least 1 hour. Drain the fish. Put the oatmeal, salt, pepper, mace and fennel seed into a bag, then toss the fish in the mixture to coat it thoroughly.

Heat the oil in a large skillet, and stir-fry the fish over moderate heat for 5 minutes, then remove from the pan.

Fry the onion, garlic, peppers and celery in the pan for 4-5 minutes, stirring frequently. Return the fish to the pan, stir in the nuts, oats and parsley, and cook for 2 minutes. Serve hot, garnished with the orange rind.

Note Lowfat yogurt swirled over the fish is a good "extra".

LONELY SHEPHERD

¾ lb lean lamb, ground
1 large onion, chopped
4 stalks celery, thinly sliced
¾ cup rolled oats
1½ cups mushrooms, sliced
6 oz canned pimientos, drained and chopped
14 oz canned tomatoes
⅔ cup tomato juice
1 tablespoon Worcestershire sauce
1 tablespoon concentrated tomato paste

1 teaspoon mixed dried herbs
salt, freshly ground pepper

TOPPING

1 lb potatoes, peeled
salt, freshly ground pepper
2 tablespoons sunflower margarine
3 tablespoons skim milk
1 large carrot, grated
½ cup Wensleydale **or** Caerphilly cheese, crumbled

Fry the lamb in a nonstick pan over moderate heat, stirring frequently, to melt the fat. Lift out the meat with a slotted spoon. Discard all but 2 teaspoons of the fat.

Cook the onion and celery in the pan for 3 minutes, stirring frequently. Add the meat and all the remaining ingredients, seasoning the mixture well with salt and pepper. Turn the mixture into a baking dish.

To make the topping, cook the potatoes in boiling, salted water until tender, then drain and mash them with the margarine and milk. Beat in the grated carrot and cheese and season with salt and pepper.

Spread the potato topping over the meat mixture, and level the surface. Stand the dish on a baking sheet, and bake in a moderately hot oven, 375°F, for 35-40 minutes until the topping is well-browned. Serve hot.

SPINACH AND VEAL ROLLS

4 veal scallops, flattened
2 tablespoons sunflower oil
1 tablespoon whole wheat flour
⅔ cup dry white wine
salt, freshly ground pepper
4 tablespoons Greek-style yogurt
parsley sprigs

FILLING

1 tablespoon sunflower oil

1 small onion, chopped
1 clove garlic, crushed
⅔ cup cooked spinach, well-drained and chopped
6 tablespoons chopped walnuts
3 tablespoons jumbo oats
2 tablespoons grated Parmesan cheese
salt, freshly ground pepper
a pinch of grated nutmeg

Make the filling first. Heat the oil in a pan, and cook the onion and garlic over moderate heat for 3 minutes, stirring once or twice. Put the spinach into a bowl, then beat in the onion mixture, the walnuts, oats and the cheese. Season with salt, pepper and nutmeg.

Divide the filling between the veal scallops. Roll up the meat to enclose the filling, and tie the rolls with string.

Heat the remaining oil in a skillet, and fry the rolls over moderate heat, turning them frequently, until evenly browned. Remove the meat from the pan.

Stir the flour into the pan, and pour on the wine, stirring constantly. Heat to the boiling point, then season with salt and pepper. Return the veal rolls to the pan, cover and simmer for 15 minutes, then transfer the meat to a heated serving dish.

Boil the sauce for 2 minutes until reduced, then stir in the yogurt. Season to taste, then pour a little of the sauce over the meat, and garnish with the parsley. Serve the remaining sauce separately.

CHICKEN AND VEGETABLE LOAF

SERVES 6-8

2 tablespoons sunflower margarine
1 medium onion, quartered
1 clove garlic
2 stalks celery, thinly sliced
2 zucchini, sliced
1 medium carrot, diced
1¼ lb raw chicken, ground
⅔ cup tomato juice

1 teaspoon Worcestershire sauce
½ cup rolled oats
4 tablespoons jumbo oats
salt, freshly ground pepper
1 teaspoon dried oregano
2 tablespoons chopped parsley
1 egg, beaten
2 hard-boiled eggs, sliced

Melt the margarine in a skillet, and fry the onion, garlic, celery, zucchini and carrot over moderate heat for 2-3 minutes, stirring frequently. Stir in the chicken, and cook for 3 minutes, stirring constantly. Remove the pan from the heat and stir in the tomato juice, Worcestershire sauce and oats. Season with salt and pepper, then stir in the herbs. Beat in the egg, and beat the mixture well.

Press half the mixture into a greased 2 lb loaf pan, and arrange the egg slices on top. Cover with the remaining mixture. Cover the pan with foil, and stand it in a roasting pan half-filled with warm water. Bake in a moderate oven, 350°F, for 1¼ hours. Leave to cool slightly, then pour off any liquid. Turn out the loaf onto a heated serving dish, and serve hot or cold.

CRISPY CHICKEN

2 tablespoons fine oatmeal
1 tablespoon oat bran and
oat germ (optional)
salt, freshly ground pepper
4 slices boneless chicken breast
(approximately 1¼-1½ lb)
6 tablespoons jumbo oats
3 tablespoons chopped hazelnuts
½ teaspoon ground coriander

½ teaspoon coriander seeds,
crushed
1 teaspoon dried thyme
1 egg, beaten

SAUCE

1 cup low fat yogurt
½ cup hazelnuts, chopped
2 tablespoons sweet sherry
1 teaspoon chopped parsley

Put the oatmeal, oat bran, salt and pepper into a bag, then toss the chicken slices in the mixture to coat them thoroughly. Mix together the jumbo oats, hazelnuts, ground coriander seeds and thyme. Dip the chicken first in the beaten egg and then in the oats mixture.

Fry the chicken in a nonstick pan over moderate heat for 8-10 minutes on each side. Serve hot.

Mix together the ingredients for the sauce, and use a little to garnish the chicken. Serve the rest separately.

Serve with a green vegetable and new potatoes steamed in their skins.

OPPOSITE *Crispy Chicken*

CHICKEN MOUSSAKA

3 tablespoons sunflower oil
2 medium eggplants, thinly sliced
1 medium onion, chopped
1 clove garlic, crushed
¾ lb raw chicken, ground
4 tablespoons rolled oats
2 tablespoons chopped parsley
2 tablespoons concentrated
tomato paste

⅔ cup chicken stock
salt, freshly ground pepper
3 tomatoes, skinned and sliced

TOPPING

1¼ cups lowfat yogurt
1 egg
⅔ cup cottage cheese
½ cup Edam cheese, grated
salt, freshly ground pepper

Heat the oil in a skillet, and fry the eggplant slices over moderate heat, turning once, to brown evenly on both sides. Remove from the pan.

Put the onion, garlic and chicken in the pan, and fry for 1 minute. Stir in the oats and parsley. Mix together the tomato paste and stock, pour into the pan, season with salt and pepper, and simmer until the liquid has been absorbed but the mixture is still moist.

Arrange the eggplants in a baking dish. Cover them with the chicken mixture, and arrange the sliced tomatoes on top.

Beat together the topping ingredients, then pour this over the tomatoes. Stand the dish on a baking sheet, and cook in a moderately hot oven, 375°F, for 45 minutes until bubbling. Serve hot or cold.

CHICKEN-STUFFED EGGPLANT

2 large eggplants
salt, freshly ground pepper
2 tablespoons sunflower oil
1 large onion, chopped
1 clove garlic, crushed
2 tablespoons concentrated
tomato paste

2½ cups cooked chicken, chopped
½ cup white wine
6 tablespoons rolled oats
2 tablespoons chopped parsley
2 tablespoons golden raisins
4 tablespoons grated cheese

Slice the eggplants in half lengthwise and criss-cross the flesh with deep cuts. Sprinkle with salt, and set aside for at least 30 minutes to draw out the bitter juices.

Meanwhile, heat the oil in a pan, and fry the onion and garlic over moderate heat for 3 minutes, stirring once or twice. Stir in the tomato paste and chicken, then pour on the wine, stirring all the time. Season with salt and pepper, and stir in 2 tablespoons of the oats. Simmer for 5 minutes until the mixture has formed a thick paste. Stir in the parsley, and remove from the heat.

Press the eggplants between your thumb and fingers to extract the moisture. Rinse them in cold water, then pat dry. Spread the chicken mixture over the vegetables. Mix the remaining oats with the golden raisins and cheese, and sprinkle this over the chicken. Press the topping down firmly. Place the eggplant halves in a baking dish, and bake in a moderately hot oven, 375°F, for 50 minutes until bubbling. Serve hot.

Serve with brown rice and a green salad.

CHICKEN WITH WATERCRESS STUFFING

SERVES 4-6

3¼ lb whole chicken including giblets
1 tablespoon lemon juice
salt, freshly ground pepper
1¼ cups chicken stock (made from
chicken giblets)
2 tablespoons orange juice
1 teaspoon grated orange rind

STUFFING

1 bunch of watercress, trimmed and
chopped (reserve a few sprigs to garnish)
4 scallions, finely chopped

1 stalk of tender celery, finely chopped
2 tablespoons chopped parsley
½ cup rolled oats
3 tablespoons orange juice
2 teaspoons grated orange
rind
a pinch of ground ginger
⅓ cup seedless raisins
salt, freshly ground pepper
4 tablespoons lowfat yogurt
1 egg, beaten

Mix together the ingredients for the stuffing, binding them with the egg.

Pack the stuffing into the chicken, and close the vents with skewers. Rub the skin all over with lemon juice, and season with black pepper. Place the chicken on a rack in a roasting pan. Cover with foil, and roast in a moderately hot oven, 375°F, for 1¼ hours. Remove the foil, and cook for an additional 15 minutes. Transfer to a heated serving dish.

Pour off and discard the fat in the pan. Pour in the chicken stock and orange juice. Add the orange rind, and season with salt and pepper. Stir well, then heat the sauce to the boiling point and boil for 3 minutes. Skim off any fat from the surface. Serve the sauce separately.

PHEASANT WITH OATMEAL STUFFING

SERVES 4-6

2 pheasants
2 tablespoons sunflower margarine,
melted
2 tablespoons fine oatmeal

STUFFING

⅔ cup medium oatmeal

1 small onion, chopped
4 tablespoons chopped parsley
3 tablespoons sunflower margarine,
melted
a pinch of grated nutmeg
salt, freshly ground pepper

Prepare the stuffing first. Mix together the oatmeal, onion, parsley, margarine, nutmeg and seasoning, and pack the stuffing into the birds.

Place the pheasants in a roasting pan. Pour the melted margarine over them, and cover with foil. Roast in a moderately hot oven, 400°F, for 40 minutes. Remove the foil and rub the oatmeal over the skin of the birds. Roast, uncovered, for an additional 10 minutes to crisp the skin.

CANNELLONI ROLLS

8 large whole wheat cannelloni tubes
1 medium onion
1 red pepper
salt, freshly ground pepper
¾ cup lowfat cottage cheese
¾ cup cooked chicken, chopped
1 tablespoon concentrated
tomato paste

2 tablespoons chopped parsley
8 stuffed green olives, chopped
½ cup chopped walnuts
5 tablespoons rolled oats
a pinch of cayenne pepper
1¼ cups lowfat yogurt
1 tablespoon lemon juice
½ cup Parmesan cheese, grated

Cook the cannelloni tubes, the onion and the pepper in boiling salted water for 4 minutes. Drain in a colander, rinse under cold water, then drain again. Pat the pasta dry with paper towels. Finely chop the onion. Seed and chop the pepper.

Beat the cottage cheese until smooth. Beat in the chopped onion and pepper, the chicken, 2 teaspoons of the tomato paste, the parsley, olives, walnuts and 3 tablespoons of the oats. Season with salt, pepper and cayenne pepper. Spoon the filling into the pasta tubes, packing it in tightly. Arrange the pasta in a greased, shallow baking dish.

Mix together the yogurt, lemon juice and remaining tomato paste, and season with salt and pepper. Pour this over the pasta, mix together the cheese and remaining oats, and sprinkle over the pasta. Bake in a moderately hot oven, 375°F, for 35 minutes until browned and bubbling. Serve hot.

Note A green salad is a cool contrast to this creamy dish. If you prefer a hot vegetable, leaf spinach is a good choice.

SQUASH BOAT

SERVES 4-6

3 lb whole butternut squash, pared

FILLING AND SAUCE

1 tablespoon sunflower oil
1 medium onion, chopped
¾ lb raw chicken, ground
½ cup oat groats, cooked
1½ cups mushrooms, chopped

1 tablespoon concentrated
tomato paste
2 teaspoons dried mixed herbs
6 stuffed olives, chopped
a pinch of grated nutmeg
salt, freshly ground pepper
2 teaspoons lemon juice
14 oz canned tomatoes, chopped

Cut a slice from each end of the squash. Use a vegetable ball scoop and, working from each end, scoop out the seeds and fibers to leave a clear channel throughout.

To make the filling, heat the oil in a pan, and cook the onion over moderate heat for 3 minutes, stirring frequently. Stir in the chicken, groats and mushrooms, and cook for 3 minutes. Stir in the tomato paste, half the herbs and the olives, and season with the nutmeg and salt and pepper. Cook for 1 minute, then add half the lemon juice. Leave to cool slightly.

Pack the filling into the squash. Stir the remaining herbs and lemon juice into the tomatoes, and season well with salt and pepper. Pour into a baking dish, place the squash on top, and cover the dish with foil. Bake in a moderately hot oven, 375°F, for 1½ hours or until the squash is tender.

Note You can bake potatoes in the oven for part of the time, and serve them topped with cottage cheese.

The Supporting Role

Creamy fennel with a crispy cheese topping; melt-in-the-mouth artichoke "boats" filled with green pea purée; golden brown pyramids of piped potato; baked onions brimful with a vegetable and nut filling; a salad ring with a spicy, curried dressing; stir-fried sprouted grains with spring vegetables: whatever – apart from being vegetable-based – can all these dishes have in common? The answer, of course, is oats; but the ways in which the cereal is used are many and various.

Additionally, oat groats may be cooked and served "plain", as is brown rice, or transformed into a colorful risotto with the addition of diced vegetables, meat, seafood and herbs. In much the same way, cooked oat groats tossed with salad, dried fruits and vegetables, or just with herbs, and served cold make a substantial salad. And for good measure, rolled oats and coarse oatmeal make a crunchy contribution to salad dressings.

You can try your hand at indoor gardening – as children love to do – and start the oat groats along the way to germination. After only four or five days the result is a jar of crisp and crunchy shoots, like Chinese beansprouts, highly nutritious and, with their slightly spicy flavor, surprisingly delicious.

Rolled oats and oatmeal can be used to good effect with vegetable purées, thickening any mixture that is too "slack" to hold its shape for piping. The cereals are invaluable, too, for absorbing any excess moisture in, for example, mashed rutabaga, which is notorious for its habit of weeping, no matter how carefully you drain it.

Add on all the crispy toppings, cheesy sauces and tasty fillings for vegetable cases, and you have to give oats full marks for the important supporting role they play, as accompaniments to the main attraction, or, if you like, the main attraction itself.

LEEKS IN WHITE WINE

1 tablespoon olive oil
4 tablespoons white wine
8 small leeks, sliced
salt, freshly ground pepper

TOPPING

4 tablespoons rolled oats, toasted
2 tablespoons chopped walnuts
2 tablespoons chopped parsley

Heat the oil and wine in a pan to the boiling point. Add the leeks, and season with salt and pepper. Simmer for about 3 minutes until the leeks are only just tender.

Mix together the ingredients for the topping, and sprinkle over the cooked leeks. Serve at once.

POTATO PYRAMIDS

SERVES 6

1 lb potatoes, peeled
salt, freshly ground pepper
2 tablespoons sunflower margarine
2 tablespoons lowfat yogurt
a pinch of turmeric
1 egg, beaten
6 tablespoons rolled oats

Cook the potatoes in boiling salted water until tender, then drain them, reserving the liquid. Mash them with 2 tablespoons of the reserved liquid, the margarine and yogurt. Season with salt, pepper and turmeric, then beat in the egg, and stir in the oats. Beat the mixture well until firm and smooth.

Spoon the potato mixture into a strong piping bag with a large, plain nozzle. Pipe a 2½ inch circle of potato on a greased baking sheet, and, piping in spiral fashion, build it up to a pyramid shape. Continue making pyramids with the remaining mixture. Bake in a moderately hot oven, 375°F, for 15 minutes or until the tips are well-browned. Serve at once.

Note The potato mixture can be left to cool, then reheated just before serving.

HIGHLAND POTATOES

4 large baking potatoes, scrubbed
2 tablespoons sunflower margarine
1 small onion, chopped
1½ cups button mushrooms, sliced
3 tablespoons jumbo oats

4 tablespoons skim milk
2 eggs, separated
salt, freshly ground pepper
2 tablespoons chopped parsley

Prick the potatoes all over with a fork to prevent the skins from bursting. Bake them in a moderately hot oven, 375°F, for 1¼ hours or until soft.

Meanwhile, melt the margarine in a pan, and cook the onion for 3-4 minutes. Add the mushrooms, and cook for an additional 2 minutes. Stir in the oats, then remove the pan from the heat.

Halve the potatoes lengthwise. Scoop out the centers, taking care not to pierce the skins. Mash the potato and beat in the milk and egg yolks. Stir in the oat mixture, and season with salt and pepper. Whisk the egg whites until stiff, then fold them into the mixture. Stir in the chopped parsley.

Fill the potato shells with the mixture, then place them on a baking sheet, and return to the oven. Bake in a moderately hot oven, 375°F, for 15 minutes until bubbling. Serve hot.

OATY POTATOES

1½ lb small new potatoes
salt
1 egg
2 tablespoons skim milk
fine oatmeal for dusting
¾ cup jumbo oats (approx)
oil for brushing

GARNISH

parsley sprigs

Cook the potatoes in boiling salted water until just tender, then drain and leave to cool.

Beat together the egg and milk. Toss the potatoes first in the fine oatmeal to coat them, and then in the egg and milk. Lift them out, draining off any excess egg, then roll in half the jumbo oats to coat them completely. Use the remaining oats to roll the potatoes a second time.

Brush a nonstick pan with oil, and heat it, then cook the potatoes over moderate heat for 4-5 minutes, turning them frequently until brown on all sides. Garnish with sprigs of parsley. Serve at once.

OAT CROQUETTES

1 lb potatoes, peeled
salt, freshly ground pepper
3 tablespoons sunflower margarine
2-4 tablespoons skim milk
4 tablespoons lowfat yogurt
1 teaspoon grated orange rind
6 tablespoons rolled oats
oil for brushing

COATING

1 egg
2 tablespoons skim milk
4 tablespoons fine oatmeal
3½ tablespoons coarse oatmeal

Cook the potatoes in boiling salted water until tender, then drain and mash them. Beat in the margarine, milk, yogurt and orange rind, then stir in the oats, and season with salt and pepper. Divide the mixture into 12 portions, and shape each one into a sausage shape.

Beat together the egg and milk. Toss the croquettes first in the fine oatmeal to coat them thoroughly, and then in the egg and milk to cover them on all sides. Lift them out, draining off any excess, then toss in the coarse oatmeal, and press it well into the surface. Leave until firm.

Brush a skillet with oil, and fry the croquettes over moderate heat for about 6 minutes, turning frequently with a wooden spoon to brown them evenly on all sides. Serve hot.

OPPOSITE *Oaty Potatoes* and *Oat Croquettes*

BAKED RUTABAGAS

1½ lb rutabagas, peeled and cubed
salt, freshly ground pepper
2 tablespoons rolled oats
6 tablespoons lowfat yogurt
a pinch of grated nutmeg
8 scallions, thinly sliced

2 tablespoons chopped parsley

TOPPING

½ cup Gruyère **or** Edam cheese, grated
⅓ cup medium oatmeal
2 tablespoons jumbo oats

Cook the rutabagas in boiling salted water for 20 minutes or until just tender. Drain and mash them, then beat in the rolled oats – they will absorb any excess moisture. Beat in the yogurt, and season with salt, pepper and nutmeg. Stir in the scallions and parsley, then transfer the mixture to a greased baking dish.

Mix together the ingredients for the topping, and sprinkle this over the rutabaga mixture. Bake in a moderately hot oven, 375°F, for 35 minutes until the topping is crisp and brown. Serve hot.

PARSNIPS WITH TOASTED OATS

1 lb parsnips, diced
salt, freshly ground pepper
4 tablespoons lowfat yogurt
¼ teaspoon grated nutmeg

TOPPING

4 tablespoons jumbo oats
2 tablespoons chopped hazelnuts

GARNISH

parsley sprigs

Prepare the topping first. Mix the oats and hazelnuts, and broil under moderate heat for 4-5 minutes, stirring once or twice to brown the mixture evenly.

Cook the diced parsnips in boiling salted water for 20-25 minutes until very tender. Drain and mash them, then return the pan to moderate heat to evaporate the excess moisture. Beat in the yogurt, then season with nutmeg, salt and pepper.

Spread the mashed parsnip mixture in a heated serving dish. Sprinkle the oats mixture on top, and garnish with the parsley. Serve at once.

VEGETABLE BURGERS

¾ lb potatoes, peeled
¾ lb parsnips
salt, freshly ground pepper
2 tablespoons sunflower margarine
1 medium onion, chopped
1 clove garlic, crushed
1 teaspoon curry powder

4 tablespoons skim milk
1 tablespoon chopped parsley
½ cup chopped hazelnuts
½ cup rolled oats
2 tablespoons sesame seeds
a pinch of grated nutmeg

Cook the potatoes and parsnips in boiling salted water until tender, then drain and mash them.

Meanwhile melt the margarine in a pan, and cook the onion and garlic over moderate heat for 3 minutes, stirring once or twice. Stir in the curry powder, and cook for 1 minute.

Beat the onion mixture into the mashed vegetables. Beat in the milk until it has been absorbed, then beat in the parsley and half the hazelnuts, oats and sesame seeds. Season the mixture with salt, pepper and nutmeg. Divide it into eight equal pieces, and shape them into balls. Press flat to make burger shapes.

Mix together the remaining nuts, oats and sesame seeds. Turn the vegetable burgers in this mixture, pressing it well into the surface. Place them on a greased baking sheet, and bake in a moderately hot oven, 375°F, for 25 minutes or until well-browned.

Variation
If preferred, the burgers can be dry-fried in a nonstick pan.

CAULIFLOWER CROWN

1 medium cauliflower
salt

DRESSING

2 tablespoons sunflower oil
1 tablespoon cider vinegar
½ teaspoon lemon juice
½ teaspoon dry English mustard

salt, freshly ground pepper

GARNISH

2 tablespoons sunflower margarine
4 tablespoons jumbo oats
2 hard-boiled eggs
1 medium onion, chopped
2 tablespoons chopped parsley

Cook the cauliflower in boiling salted water for 10-15 minutes until just tender, then drain well. Transfer to a heated serving dish, cover with foil and keep warm.

Meanwhile, mix together the ingredients for the dressing, and make the garnish. Melt the margarine in a pan, and fry the oats over moderate heat for 3-4 minutes, stirring constantly, until dry and toasted. Chop the egg whites. Sieve the yolks.

Pour the dressing over the cauliflower, then arrange rings of oats, egg white, egg yolk, chopped onion and parsley over the cauliflower. Serve at once.

VEGETABLE RAMEKINS

¼ medium cauliflower
3 carrots
1½ cups peas
salt, freshly ground pepper
9 tablespoons lowfat yogurt
a pinch of grated nutmeg
1 teaspoon grated orange rind

1 tablespoon chopped mint **or**
1 teaspoon dried mint

TOPPING

4 tablespoons rolled oats
4 tablespoons grated Parmesan
cheese

Cook the cauliflower, carrots and peas in separate pans of boiling salted water until tender. Drain the vegetables and mash each type separately. Season each purée with salt and pepper, then beat in 3 tablespoons of the yogurt. Add the grated nutmeg to the cauliflower purée. Beat the orange rind into the carrot purée. Beat the mint into the pea purée.

Make layers of the cauliflower, carrot and pea purées in four greased individual ramekin dishes.

Mix together the oats and cheese for the topping, and sprinkle over each dish. Cover with foil, and stand the dishes in a roasting pan half-filled with boiling water. Bake them in a moderately hot oven, 375°F, for 20 minutes. Serve hot.

Note This dish makes an unusual and colorful first course, or a three-in-one vegetable accompaniment to roast or broiled meat and poultry.

HIGH-FIBER ONIONS

4 large Spanish onions
(approximately 1½ lb)
¾ cup whole wheat bread crumbs
4 tablespoons coarse oatmeal
1 tablespoon chopped parsley
1 teaspoon dried oregano
½ cup cashew nuts, chopped
⅓ cup currants
3 tablespoons orange juice

2 teaspoons grated orange rind
salt, freshly ground pepper
4 tablespoons Greek-style yogurt

TOPPING

2 tablespoons jumbo oats
4 tablespoons grated Parmesan
cheese

Cook the onions in boiling water for 7 minutes, then drain and dry them. Open out the onions from the center and, using a teaspoon, scoop out the centers, leaving firm "walls". Place the onions in a baking dish. Chop the onion centers.

Mix together the chopped onion, bread crumbs, oatmeal, herbs, nuts, currants, orange juice and orange rind. Season the mixture with salt and pepper, then stir in the yogurt. Pack the mixture into the onion shells.

Mix together the jumbo oats and cheese for the topping, and sprinkle on top of the filling. Bake in a moderately hot oven, 375°F, for 30 minutes until brown and bubbling. Serve at once, with roast or broiled poultry.

PEA-GREEN BOATS

1 ½ cups fresh peas
2 tablespoons sunflower margarine
4 tablespoons chicken stock
1 small onion, finely chopped
salt, freshly ground pepper
4 tablespoons fine oatmeal

1 tablespoon lowfat yogurt
2 tablespoons chopped mint
1 ½ lb canned artichoke bottoms,
drained
mint sprigs

Put the peas in a pan with the margarine, stock and onion. Season with salt and pepper. Heat to the boiling point, then cover the pan and simmer for 10 minutes or until the peas are tender and have absorbed most of the stock.

Purée the peas and any stock in a blender or press through a sieve. Blend in the oatmeal, yogurt and mint, then season to taste.

Arrange the artichoke bottoms in a greased, shallow baking dish, and spoon or pipe in the pea purée. Bake the artichokes in a moderate oven, 350°F, for 10 minutes until bubbling. Garnish with the mint sprigs, and serve hot.

BRAISED VEGETABLES

2 tablespoons olive oil
1 teaspoon lemon juice
6 tablespoons white wine
3 tablespoons concentrated
tomato paste
1 medium onion, thinly sliced
2 cloves garlic, finely chopped
1 teaspoon coriander seeds
½ teaspoon mustard seeds

2 dried red chili peppers
2 bay leaves
salt, freshly ground pepper
½ lb pearl onions
4 stalks celery, cut into 1 ½ inch slices
2 ¼ cups button mushrooms, sliced
½ small cauliflower, cut into florets
4 tablespoons jumbo oats
2 tablespoons chopped parsley

Put the oil, lemon juice, wine, tomato paste, onion, garlic, seeds, chili peppers, bay leaves and seasoning into a pan, stir well and heat to the boiling point. Cover the pan and simmer for 20 minutes. Add the pearl onions, celery, mushrooms and cauliflower florets, and return to the boiling point. Cover and cook for 15 minutes, then stir in the jumbo oats. Season to taste, then cook for an additional 5 minutes. Discard the bay leaves. Stir in the parsley. Serve warm, as an accompaniment to roast or broiled meats.

Variation
The recipe can be chilled and served, Greek style, as an appetizer.

FENNEL IN CHEESE SAUCE

3 medium bulbs fennel, sliced
salt, freshly ground pepper

SAUCE

2 tablespoons sunflower margarine
2½ tablespoons fine oatmeal
1 scant cup buttermilk
½ cup lowfat cottage cheese
2 tablespoons chopped parsley
a pinch of grated nutmeg

TOPPING

½ cup jumbo oats
½ cup Gruyère **or** Edam cheese, grated

GARNISH (optional)

sprays of fennel leaves

Cook the fennel in boiling salted water for about 5 minutes or until just tender. Drain thoroughly (reserving the stock for a sauce or soup), and pat dry. Arrange in a greased, shallow baking dish.

To make the sauce, melt the margarine in a pan, and stir in the oatmeal until it forms a smooth paste. Stir in the buttermilk, stirring constantly, and heat to the boiling point, then simmer for 3 minutes. Beat in the cheese and parsley, a little at a time, then season with salt, pepper and nutmeg. Pour the sauce over the fennel.

Mix together the oats and cheese for the topping, and sprinkle this over the sauce. Bake in a moderate oven, 350°F, for 20 minutes until brown and bubbling. Garnish, if desired, with the fennel leaves. Serve hot.

CRISPY BRUSSELS SPROUTS

1 lb Brussels sprouts
salt, freshly ground pepper
2 tablespoons orange juice
1 teaspoon grated orange rind
2 tablespoons lowfat yogurt

TOPPING

1 tablespoon sunflower margarine
2 tablespoons sunflower oil
1 small onion, finely chopped
4 tablespoons jumbo oats
4 tablespoons chopped walnuts

Steam the Brussels sprouts over boiling salted water for 12-15 minutes or until barely tender.

Mix together the orange juice, orange rind and yogurt, and season with salt and pepper. Simmer the vegetables in the sauce for 2-3 minutes until the liquid has almost evaporated.

To make the topping, heat the margarine and oil in a pan, and cook the onion over moderate heat for 2 minutes, stirring frequently. Add the oats and walnuts, and cook over moderate heat for 2-3 minutes, stirring all the time. Sprinkle the topping over the vegetables, and serve at once.

BAKED AVOCADOS

2 medium avocados, halved and pitted
2 teaspoons lemon juice
⅔ cup lowfat cream cheese
2 medium cooked carrots, diced
2 tablespoons jumbo oats
½ cup chopped walnuts

1 teaspoon snipped chives
salt, freshly ground pepper

GARNISH

parsley sprigs
walnut halves

Brush the cut surfaces of the avocados with the lemon juice. Beat the cheese until soft, then stir in the carrots, oats, walnuts and chives. Season with salt and pepper. Divide the filling between the avocado halves. Wrap each one in foil, and place in a shallow baking dish. Bake in a moderately hot oven, 375°F, for 20 minutes until bubbling. Serve at once, garnished with the parsley sprigs and walnuts.

Note This unusual, hot avocado dish is good with baked or broiled fish, or with white meat such as chicken and veal. It also makes an attractive appetizer.

OAT BIRIANI

SERVES 4-6

1⅛ cups oat groats, soaked and drained
2 tablespoons sunflower oil
2 medium onions, thinly sliced
2 cloves garlic, crushed
2 stalks celery, thinly sliced
½ teaspoon turmeric
½ teaspoon ground ginger
½ teaspoon ground cumin
¼ teaspoon cayenne pepper
salt

1 tablespoon concentrated
tomato paste
⅔ cups hot chicken stock
2 medium carrots, diced
½ small cauliflower, cut into florets
1½ cups button mushrooms, thinly sliced
2 large tomatoes, skinned and chopped
½ cup seedless raisins
½ cup blanched almonds

GARNISH

lemon wedges

Cook the groats in boiling unsalted water for 1 hour, then drain them.

Heat the oil in a pan, and fry the onions, garlic and celery over moderate heat for 2 minutes. Stir in the spices and salt, and cook for 1 minute, then add the tomato paste and stock, stirring constantly. Add the drained groats, the carrots and cauliflower, heat to the boiling point, then cover and simmer for 10 minutes. Add the mushrooms and tomatoes, and cook for an additional 3-4 minutes. Stir in the raisins, and heat through. Scatter the almonds on top. Serve hot, garnished with the lemon wedges.

Note This is a good accompaniment to spiced meat dishes or to vegetable kabobs.

CURRIED OAT RING

SERVES 6-8

1 scant cup oat groats, soaked and
drained
6 oz canned pimientos, drained and
sliced
1 green pepper, seeded and chopped
3 tomatoes, skinned, seeded and
chopped
3 scallions, chopped
4 tablespoons golden raisins
8 dried apricots, chopped
2 tablespoons seedless raisins
2 tablespoons blanched chopped
almonds

oil for brushing
DRESSING

2 tablespoons sunflower oil
2 tablespoons red wine vinegar
1 tablespoon lemon juice
1 teaspoon curry powder
1 clove garlic, crushed
2 tablespoons lowfat yogurt
salt, freshly ground pepper

Cook the groats in boiling water for 1¼-1½ hours, then drain thoroughly and rinse under cold running water. Drain again, then leave to cool.

Cut one pimiento slice into ½ inch diamond shapes, and set aside. Chop the remainder, then mix together with the groats, pepper, tomatoes, scallions, dried fruit and almonds.

Mix together the ingredients for the dressing until well-blended, and pour this over the groats mixture.

Brush a 2½ cup ring mold with oil. Arrange the reserved pimiento diamond shapes in the base. Pack the oat salad into the mold, then cover and chill for at least 1½ hours.

Run a knife blade around the inside of the mold, and turn out onto a serving plate.

Serve with other salads or to accompany cold or broiled meats.

OPPOSITE *Green Salad with Oat Dressing, Bean Salad (page 78) and Curried Oat Ring*

GREEN SALAD WITH OAT DRESSING

SERVES 6

1 small curly endive
1 head chicory
1 bulb fennel, thinly sliced
4 scallions, thinly sliced
1 small cucumber, thinly sliced

DRESSING

3 tablespoons olive oil
3 tablespoons cider vinegar
2 tablespoons lowfat yogurt
¼ teaspoon dry English mustard
salt, freshly ground pepper
3 tablespoons jumbo oats

Prepare the dressing first. Mix together the oil, vinegar, yogurt and mustard until well-blended. Season with salt and pepper, then stir in the oats. Put aside for at least 1 hour.

   Meanwhile, discard the outer leaves of the endive and chicory. Tear off each leaf, and tear in half any very large ones. Toss together the endive, chicory, fennel, onions and cucumber. If the salad is to be stored before serving, put it in a plastic bag in the refrigerator.

   Just before serving, pour the dressing over the salad, and toss to coat the leaves thoroughly. Serve in a chilled bowl.

EGGPLANT SALAD WITH OAT DRESSING

SERVES 4-6

1 large eggplant
1 medium zucchini, thinly sliced
1½ cups button mushrooms, thinly sliced

DRESSING

5 tablespoons lowfat yogurt
3 tablespoons orange juice

2 tablespoons sunflower seeds
2 tablespoons coarse oatmeal
2 tablespoons chopped parsley
1 clove garlic, crushed
salt, freshly ground pepper

GARNISH

orange wedges

Prepare the dressing first. Beat the yogurt until smooth, then beat in the orange juice. Stir in the sunflower seeds, oatmeal, parsley and garlic, and season with salt and pepper. Set aside for at least 1 hour.

Meanwhile, prick the eggplant all over with a fork, then broil under high heat for about 20 minutes, turning frequently so that it is almost black on all sides. Hold it under cold running water, then peel off the skin and thinly slice it. Leave to cool.

Toss together the eggplant, zucchini and mushroom slices, then pour on the dressing, and toss to coat the vegetables thoroughly. Garnish with the orange wedges.

Note This salad makes a good accompaniment to broiled lamb dishes, such as kabobs.

OAT SALAD WITH ZUCCHINI

6 zucchini, thinly sliced
salt
¾ cup oat groats, cooked
4 medium tomatoes, skinned and chopped
2 tablespoons pumpkin seeds
6 stuffed olives, chopped
lemon wedges

DRESSING

3 tablespoons olive oil
2 tablespoons red wine vinegar
1 tablespoon chopped mint
1 teaspoon chopped basil **or**
½ teaspoon dried basil
salt, freshly ground pepper

Blanch the zucchini slices in salted water for 2 minutes, then drain them and pat dry. Leave to cool.

Meanwhile, mix together the ingredients for the dressing until well-blended.

Toss together the cooled zucchini slices, the groats, tomatoes, pumpkin seeds and olives. Pour on the dressing, and toss well. Garnish with the lemon wedges.

Note Serve this vegetable and oat dish as part of a salad meal or to accompany broiled fish or meats.

GREEN OAT SALAD

SERVES 4-6

I scant cup oat groats, soaked and drained
3 cups parsley, chopped
spinach **or** lettuce leaves
4 large tomatoes, sliced

DRESSING

3 tablespoons olive oil
4 tablespoons lemon juice

I teaspoon grated lemon rind
2 cloves garlic, crushed
6 scallions, thinly sliced
salt, freshly ground pepper

GARNISH

lemon slices

Cook the oat groats in boiling water for 1¼-1½ hours, then drain thoroughly and rinse under cold running water. Drain again, then toss the oats on a tea towel to dry them well. Leave to cool.

Meanwhile, prepare the dressing. Mix together the oil, lemon juice, lemon rind and garlic. Stir in the scallions, and season with salt and pepper.

Stir together the groats and parsley, pour on the dressing, and mix well.

Line a serving dish with spinach or lettuce leaves. Pile the salad in the center, and arrange the tomato slices around the outside. Garnish with the lemon slices.

Note Serve as part of a cold meal or as a vegetarian appetizer.

SPROUTED OATS

You can make crisp, crunchy salad shoots, like bean shoots, by germinating oat grains. The sprouts are not only rich in proteins and vitamins — especially Vitamin C which is not present in the ungerminated grain — they are also delicious!

3 tablespoons oat groats
warm water

Soak the oat groats overnight in a bowl of warm water, then drain. Place the seeds in a 2 lb preserving jar, and fill with warm water. Cover the jar with a piece of cheesecloth or similar material, and secure it with a rubber band or string. Shake the jar and drain off the water. Put the jar on its side in a dark place, such as a drawer.

Fill the jar with warm water each day, shake well, drain off the water, and return to a dark place. The groats should sprout in about 5 days.

Use the sprouted oats when the shoots are about 1 inch long.

Serve raw with other salad ingredients, stir-fry with vegetables or steam over boiling stock.

Note Sprouted oats *must* be served crisp.

STIR-FRIED OATS

½ lb snow peas
salt
2 tablespoons peanut oil
2 thin slices fresh ginger root, finely
chopped
4 scallions, thinly sliced
2 cloves garlic, finely chopped
4 stalks tender celery, thinly sliced
2 cups sprouted oats (page 77)
1 cup cashew nuts

SAUCE

1 tablespoon soy sauce
2 tablespoons medium sherry
2 tablespoons chicken stock
freshly ground pepper
a pinch of ground ginger

Blanch the snow peas in boiling salted water for 2 minutes, then drain and pat dry.
    Mix together the ingredients for the sauce.
    Heat the oil in a heavy-based pan or wok, and stir-fry the ginger, onions, garlic and
celery over high heat for 30 seconds. Add the snow peas and sprouted oats, and stir-fry for
1 minute. Pour on the sauce, heat to the boiling point, stirring constantly, then simmer for
2 minutes. Stir in the cashew nuts. Serve at once.

BEAN SALAD

SERVES 6

⅔ cup dried red kidney beans, soaked
and drained (see **Note**)
½ cup dried black **or** flageolet beans,
soaked and drained (see **Note**)
4 cups sprouted oats (page 77)
2 stalks celery, thinly sliced
onion rings
parsley sprigs

DRESSING

3 tablespoons sunflower oil
3 tablespoons orange juice
1 teaspoon lemon juice
¼ teaspoon dry English mustard
1 clove garlic, crushed
salt, freshly ground pepper

Boil the kidney beans and the black beans briskly in separate pans of fresh water for 10
minutes, then cook for 1 hour or until tender.
    Meanwhile, mix together the ingredients for the dressing until well-blended.
    Drain the cooked beans, mix them together, and toss at once in the dressing. Leave to
cool.
    Stir the sprouted oats and celery into the cooled beans, then transfer the salad to a
serving dish. Scatter with the onion rings, and garnish with the parsley sprigs.

Note It is important to discard the draining water used for soaking the dried beans.

A "Sweet" Tooth

There's no doubt about it that it's the dessert course that presents the most difficulty in a healthy eating plan: if you choose to have a prepared dessert at all, that is. It has to be said that you can't beat a selection of fresh fruits – those delicious, colorful, tempting all-shapes-and-sizes packages of nutrition, fiber and flavor. But there are times when family and friends, the cook too, like to round off a meal with "something for a change".

This chapter looks on the bright side, at the various types of desserts that will satisfy the "sweet tooths" among us, without devastating the calorie bank.

Dried fruits of all kinds are an absolute boon, packed as they are with natural fruit sugars; fiber, too. Most dried fruits have approximately ten times the fiber content, weight for weight, of their fresh counterparts.

Borrow this extra-sweetness of dried apricots, peaches, pears and dates by mixing them with tangy fresh fruits. Make a light purée of dried fruits, and poach sliced apples or pears in it; no need for sugar then. And you can even dry dates until they are drier still, and grind them to a coarse powder which is a very acceptable sugar substitute (see recipe on page 89).

And where do oats come in? Tossed with berries into whipped yogurt to simulate a Scottish favorite; layered in a summer pudding to soak up the full flavor of the berry juices; stirred into simmered berries to thicken them until they "sway"; as crunchy and cobbler toppings; fillings for apples and peaches; and even blended with yogurt in a dairy dressing to serve with broiled fruit kabobs.

LOWLAND CROWDIE

4 tablespoons medium oatmeal
4 tablespoons jumbo **or** rolled oats
1¼ cups lowfat yogurt
1 tablespoon clear honey, melted
1¾ cups raspberries, hulled

Toast the oatmeal and the oats separately under moderate heat for about 4 minutes, stirring frequently, until evenly brown. Leave to cool.

Beat the yogurt until smooth, and stir in the honey, most of the raspberries and the cooled oatmeal. Divide the mixture between four individual serving dishes, sprinkle the toasted oats on top, and decorate with the reserved raspberries.

OAT FRUMENTY

SERVES 6

I scant cup oat groats, soaked and
drained
2½ cups skim milk
2 eggs
I tablespoon clear honey
⅔ cup seedless raisins
2 teaspoons lemon rind
¼ teaspoon ground mace
a pinch of grated nutmeg

Cook the groats in boiling water for 1¼ hours, then drain thoroughly, rinse under cold running water, and drain again. Put the groats into a greased 10 inch pie dish.

Beat together the milk, eggs and honey, and pour this over the groats. Stir in the raisins, lemon rind, mace and nutmeg. Bake in a moderately slow oven, 325°F, for 1 hour until set. Serve hot or cold.

Note A drizzle of honey on top is traditional with this simple pudding which dates back to Roman times.

BLACK CURRANT KISSEL

1½ lb blackcurrants, stripped from stalks
2 tablespoons water
a pinch of ground cinnamon
2 tablespoons date "sugar" (page 89) **or** clear honey
2 tablespoons fine oatmeal

DECORATION

scented geranium **or** herb leaves

Put the black currants, water, cinnamon and date "sugar" or honey in a pan. Heat slowly to boiling point, stirring occasionally to dissolve the honey.

Stir a little of the juice from the pan into the oatmeal to make a thick paste. Add more, stirring constantly, until the mixture is the consistency of light cream, then pour it into the fruit. Stir over moderate heat until the mixture thickens. Pour the fruit into a heatproof serving dish, and leave to cool. Decorate the dish with the leaves, and serve with yogurt or cottage cheese.

Variations
Other fruits are equally good cooked and served in this way. Try rhubarb, red currants, raspberries or blackberries.

FRUIT KABOBS

12 dried apricots, soaked and drained
8 prunes, pitted
1 orange, divided into segments, pith and
skin removed
2 dessert apples, cored and quartered

MARINADE

4 tablespoons orange juice
1 teaspoon grated orange rind

1 tablespoon chopped mint
1 tablespoon sunflower oil

DRESSING

½ cup cottage cheese
3 tablespoons rolled oats
4 tablespoons orange juice
1 teaspoon grated orange rind
5 tablespoons lowfat yogurt

Divide the fruit between four skewers, alternating between fresh and dried fruits and differing colors. Place the skewers in a shallow ovenproof dish.

Mix together the marinade ingredients. Pour this over the skewers, turn them to coat the fruit thoroughly, then set aside for at least 1 hour.

Meanwhile, purée the dressing ingredients in a blender. Alternatively, sieve the cheese and beat in the remaining ingredients. Chill the dressing.

Broil the skewers under moderate heat for 5-6 minutes until the fruit is well-browned. Serve at once, accompanied by the dressing.

GOLDEN FRUIT SALAD

1 teaspoon coriander seeds
2 inch piece of cinnamon stick
1 tablespoon clear honey
2½ cups water
⅔ cups white wine
12 oz mixed dried fruits, e.g., apple
rings, apricots, peaches, pears, prunes
⅓ cup seedless raisins
½ cup jumbo oats, toasted

Put the coriander seeds, cinnamon, honey and water into a pan, and heat slowly to the boiling point. Boil for 10 minutes, then add the wine and mixed dried fruit, and simmer for 1 hour until the fruit is tender. Stir in the raisins, and cook for an additional 5 minutes, then discard the cinnamon stick. Just before serving, scatter on the toasted oats. Serve hot or cold, with lowfat yogurt.

APRICOT FOLLY

1⅓ cups dried apricots, chopped, soaked and drained
⅔ cup cottage cheese
⅔ cup lowfat yogurt
¾ cup rolled oats **or** jumbo oats
2 tablespoons Amaretti liqueur (optional)

DECORATION

4 fresh apricots
8 small bay leaves

Purée the apricots with the cheese, yogurt, oats and liqueur, if used. Divide the purée between four individual glasses, and decorate each one with a fresh apricot and the bay leaves. Serve chilled, with Oat Cakes (see page 20).

Variations

You can use other well-flavored fruit purées for this smooth, satisfying dessert. Black currant purée, flavored with a little cassis, is excellent.

PRAIRIE ICEBOX DESSERT

SERVES 4-6

2 egg yolks
1¼ cups lowfat yogurt
1¼ cups apricot purée (see **Note**)
½ cups rolled oats, toasted
blanched almonds, toasted and chopped

Beat the egg yolks with the yogurt until the mixture is creamy. Gradually beat in the apricot purée, then stir in the toasted oats. Turn the mixture into a chilled container such as a 1 lb loaf pan. Cover with foil, and freeze for 1 hour.

Turn the partly frozen mixture into a chilled bowl, and beat well to break down the ice crystals. Return it to the container, cover and freeze for an additional 3 hours.

To turn out the dessert, rinse out a tea towel in warm water, wring well, and wrap around the container. Turn out the frozen dessert onto a serving dish, and press on the toasted almonds. Leave to rest in the refrigerator for 30 minutes before serving, cut in slices.

This dessert is particularly good accompanied by berries such as strawberries and raspberries.

Note Apricot purée is available in jars as baby food. Alternatively, it can be made by soaking 1 cup dried apricots, chopped, in ⅔ cup water for 2 hours, then puréeing both fruit and liquid in a blender or pressing it through a sieve.

OPPOSITE *Apricot Folly, Lowland Crowdie (page 79) and Prairie Icebox Dessert*

APPLE AND GINGER CRUNCH

1 lb cooking apples, pared, cored and
thinly sliced
¾ cup dried apricots, soaked, drained
and chopped
4 tablespoons orange juice
1 teaspoon grated orange rind

TOPPING

¾ cup whole wheat flour
2½ tablespoons medium oatmeal
1 teaspoon ground ginger
4 tablespoons sunflower margarine
2 tablespoons raw cane sugar
½ cup rolled oats
½ teaspoon coriander seeds, lightly
crushed

Put the apples, apricots, orange juice and rind into a 10 inch pie dish.

To prepare the topping, mix together the flour, oatmeal and ginger, then rub in the margarine. Stir in the sugar, rolled oats and coriander seeds. Sprinkle the mixture over the fruit, and bake in a moderately hot oven, 375°F, for 35 minutes until the topping is crisp and golden. Serve hot, warm or cold – it's equally delicious.

CIDER-BAKED APPLES

4 large cooking apples
6 tablespoons medium cider

FILLING

10 medium pitted dried dates, finely chopped
2 tablespoons jumbo oats
1 tablespoon lemon juice
1 teaspoon grated lemon rind

Core the apples, taking care to remove all the tough, inedible parts. Run a sharp knife round the center circumference of the skin to prevent the fruit from bursting. Place the apples in a baking dish that just fits them.

Mix together the dates, oats, lemon juice and lemon rind until the filling is well-blended. Pack the filling into the apples, and pile it into a dome on top.

Pour the cider over the apples, and cook them in a moderate oven, 350°F, basting them occasionally, for 45 minutes or until the apples are just beginning to soften. Do not let them collapse. Serve hot, with lowfat yogurt.

CARROT PUDDING

1 cup whole wheat bread crumbs
⅓ cup fine oatmeal
4 tablespoons rolled oats
1 cup carrots, grated
½ cup ground almonds
a pinch of grated nutmeg
½ teaspoon ground cinnamon

3 tablespoons orange juice
2 teaspoons grated orange rind
⅓ cup seedless raisins
⅓ cup golden raisins
½ cup walnuts, chopped
2 eggs, separated

Mix together the bread crumbs, oatmeal, oats, grated carrot, almonds and spices. Stir in the orange juice and rind, the raisins, golden raisins and walnuts. Beat the egg yolks, then beat them into the mixture. Whisk the egg whites until stiff, then fold them into the mixture.

Turn the mixture into a greased 4 cup pudding mold. Cover the top with foil and tie securely. Stand the mold on a trivet in a large pan with boiling water which comes halfway up the sides. Cover the pan, and boil for 1¾ hours, topping up with more boiling water as required.

Run a knife around the pudding, then turn it out carefully onto a heated serving dish. Serve hot, with lowfat yoghurt or sour cream.

SUMMER PUDDING

6 dried pears, soaked
2 cups raspberries, hulled
2 cups black currants, stripped from stalks
1 tablespoon date "sugar" (page 89) **or** clear honey
6-7 slices whole wheat bread, crusts removed
½ cup rolled oats

Cook the pears in their soaking water for 30 minutes. Drain them, and reserve 3 tablespoons of the liquid. Chop the pears.

Put the raspberries, black currants and date "sugar" or honey in a pan. Heat to the boiling point in the reserved liquid, then simmer for 5 minutes. Stir in the chopped pears.

Line a greased 2½ cup bowl with some of the bread slices, cutting them so that there are no gaps.

Set aside 4 tablespoons of the juice remaining from cooking the fruit. Fill the lined bowl with the fruit and its juice, sprinkling the oats between each "layer". Cover the top of the bowl completely with the remaining bread slices cut to fit. Place a saucer to fit inside the rim of the bowl, and stand a heavy weight on it – e.g., a filled food can. Chill overnight in the refrigerator.

Run a knife around the pudding, and turn it out onto a plate. Spoon over the reserved fruit juice to cover any unsoaked areas of bread. Cut the pudding into wedges, and serve with lowfat yogurt or sour cream.

NORTH SEA PANCAKES

1 cup whole wheat flour
salt
1¼ cups orange juice
2 eggs
1 teaspoon grated orange rind
4 tablespoons rolled oats
1⅓ cups dried apricots, chopped
oil for frying

FILLING

1 cup lowfat cottage cheese
1 tablespoon orange juice
1 teaspoon grated orange rind

DECORATION (optional)

orange wedges

Mix together the flour and salt. Gradually beat in the orange juice and then the eggs, one at a time. Stir in the orange rind, oats and apricots.

Beat the cottage cheese for the filling until smooth, then beat in the orange juice and rind.

Lightly brush a nonstick omelet pan with oil, if necessary. Heat the pan over moderate heat, and pour in just enough of the batter to cover the base. Shake the pan, and cook the batter for 2-3 minutes until it bubbles and the underside is brown. Flip or toss the pancake, and cook until the other side is brown. Keep the cooked pancake warm while cooking the remaining batter.

Spread the filling over half of each pancake. Fold them in half, and then in half again. Serve at once, accompanied, if desired, by the orange wedges.

BAKED PEACHES

SERVES 6

6 large, ripe peaches, skinned, halved and pitted

1 teaspoon grated orange rind
4 tablespoons sunflower margarine

FILLING

½ cup ground almonds
4 tablespoons rolled oats **or** jumbo oats
½ teaspoon ground cinnamon

SAUCE

2 cups raspberries, hulled
2 tablespoons clear honey

Prepare the filling first. Mix together the almonds, oats, cinnamon and orange rind, then rub in the margarine. Spread the filling over the cut sides of the peaches, packing it firmly into the cavities.

To make the sauce, heat the raspberries and honey until they just reach the boiling point, then pour the sauce into a baking dish.

Arrange the peaches, filled sides up, in the dish, and bake in a moderately hot oven, 375°F, for about 20 minutes until the filling is brown and bubbling. Serve hot.

OPPOSITE *North Sea Pancakes*

BANANA AND APPLE TART

SERVES 6

1 cup cottage cheese
½ cup rolled oats
1 teaspoon grated lemon rind
½ teaspoon ground cinnamon
2 bananas, mashed
⅓ cup dried mulberries **or** golden raisins
2 dessert apples, cored and thinly sliced
2 tablespoons clear honey, melted

OATMEAL PASTRY

1½ cups whole wheat flour
⅓ cup fine oatmeal **plus** extra for rolling
2 teaspoons baking powder
salt
1 teaspoon ground cinnamon
8 tablespoons sunflower margarine
3 tablespoons lowfat yogurt

Make the pastry first. Mix together the flour, oatmeal, baking powder, salt and cinnamon, then rub in the margarine. Stir in the yogurt, and form the mixture into a dough. Lightly dust a sheet of parchment paper with fine oatmeal. Roll out the dough to ¼ inch thickness, and use to line an 8 inch square baking pan. Trim the edges, and prick the base with a fork.

Mix together the cheese, oats, lemon rind and cinnamon. Spread the mixture over the pastry case. Mix the bananas and mulberries or golden raisins, and spread the fruit over the cheese. Arrange the apple slices in rows on top, and brush them with the melted honey. Bake in a moderately hot oven, 375°F, for 40 minutes until lightly browned. Serve cold.

Note Lowfat yogurt beaten with a mashed banana and a few drops of lemon juice makes a good accompaniment.

ATHOLL BROSE

Named after the 15th century Duke of Atholl, this dessert was originally made of thickly whipped cream spooned over the potent drink by which means he is said to have defeated his enemy.

3 cups Greek-style yogurt, chilled
4 tablespoons jumbo oats, toasted

LIQUID BASE

2½ tablespoons coarse **or** medium oatmeal
1 scant cup water
2 tablespoons clear honey
1¼ cups Scotch whisky

First make the liquid base. Soak the oatmeal in the water for about 1 hour, then press it through a fine sieve, and discard the oatmeal. Gradually pour the liquid onto the honey, stirring constantly. Pour the mixture into a jar, pour on the whisky, and shake well. Cover the bottle and store in a cool place. Shake it occasionally and always before using.

Pour 2 tablespoons of the whisky mixture into each of four individual serving glasses. Spoon on the yogurt. Scatter the toasted oats on top.

Note The liquid base can be stored in a screw-topped jar to use over several months.

RHUBARB AND PEAR COBBLER

SERVES 6

12 dried pears, soaked
1 lb rhubarb, cut into 2 inch slices
1 tablespoon date "sugar" (optional)
3 tablespoons medium oatmeal

TOPPING

1½ cups whole wheat flour
⅓ cup fine oatmeal **plus** extra for rolling

salt
½ teaspoon ground cinnamon
4 tablespoons sunflower margarine
½ cup dried mulberries **or** golden raisins
2 tablespoons raw cane sugar (optional)
⅔ cup (approximately) lowfat yogurt
milk for brushing
2 tablespoons medium oatmeal

Cook the pears in their soaking water for 30 minutes. Drain them, reserving the liquid. Put the pears, rhubarb, 4 tablespoons of the reserved juice and the date "sugar" if used, into a 10 inch pie dish. Stir in the oatmeal.

To make the topping, mix together the flour, fine oatmeal, salt and cinnamon. Rub in the margarine, then stir in the dried fruit and sugar, if used. Pour on just enough of the yogurt to make a firm dough.

Roll out the dough on a surface lightly sprinkled with fine oatmeal, to a thickness of ½ inch, and cut out the dough into circles with a 2½ inch round cutter. Re-roll the trimmings and cut out more circles. Arrange the scone circles, slightly overlapping, over the fruit. Brush with milk, then sprinkle with the medium oatmeal. Bake in a hot oven, 400°F, for 30-35 minutes until the scone topping is well risen and golden-brown. Serve hot, with lowfat yogurt or sour cream.

DATE "SUGAR"

MAKES ½ lb (approx)

You can make a high-fiber powder with the sweetness of natural sugar by drying and grinding dates.

1 lb whole dried dates, pitted

Spread the dates in a single layer, and each one separate, on a baking sheet. Bake them in a very slow oven, 250°F, for about 12 hours, turning them occasionally, until they are very hard and light in weight. They should lose about half their weight.

Grind a few dates at a time by dropping them onto the revolving blades of a blender or food processor. Store the coarse powder in an airtight container.

Note When making baked dishes soak the date "sugar" in the liquid ingredients for 10 minutes to prevent it from burning.

The Waft of Baking

Oat cakes, griddle scones, flip-and-toss pancakes, thin, flat breads like pita, and moist breads spiced with ginger have been firmly established in the oat cuisine of northern Europe where oats have flourished for so many centuries. Yet flat heavy breads were the order of the day until improved strains of wheat with rising properties were available which would withstand low temperatures and heavy rains.

Despite their many virtues, the poor rising properties of oats produce a bread with a pleasant, slightly yogurty flavor, but no bounce. Yet mixed with whole wheat flour and supplemented, if you like, with an extra rising agent, you have the best of both worlds: a loaf with the rising properties of wheat, the added flavor of oats, and both the insoluble and soluble fiber provided by the two grains.

If you are trying to restrict your fat and sugar intake, alas the Scottish flapjacks, Danish lace biscuits and lakeland gingerbreads are not for you. Try instead the soda bread flavored with cheese and herbs; the scones sweetened with fresh and dried fruits and sometimes a spoonful of date "sugar" (see page 89); the moist tea breads, which are heavenly sliced and spread with cottage cheese; the light-as-air muffins, and the plain, ordinary and very delicious oat bread – the perfect accompaniment to soups and salads.

APRICOT SCONE

MAKES 6 SLICES

4 tablespoons date "sugar" (page 89)
⅔ cup buttermilk
1½ cups whole wheat self-rising flour
⅓ cup fine oatmeal **plus** extra for dusting
2 tablespoons rolled oats
1 teaspoon baking powder

salt
¼ teaspoon allspice
3 tablespoons sunflower margarine
¾ cup dried apricots, chopped
milk for brushing

Soak the date "sugar" in the buttermilk for at least 10 minutes.

Mix together the dry ingredients. Rub in the margarine, then stir in the apricots. Pour on just enough of the sweetened buttermilk to make a firm dough.

Shape the dough into a circle on a surface lightly sprinkled with oatmeal, then press it into a 7 inch round pan. Mark into six wedges, and brush the top with milk. Bake in a hot oven, 425°F, for 20-25 minutes until well risen and golden-brown. Cool slightly in the pan, then turn out onto a wire rack. Serve warm, if possible.

Note Cottage cheese is a good "spread".

Apple Scones (*page 95*), Banana Tea Bread, Cheese and Herb Soda Bread (*page 93*) and Oat Braid (*page 92*)

BANANA TEA BREAD

MAKES ONE 7 inch SQUARE LOAF

l cup date "sugar" (page 89)
3 eggs
6 tablespoons sunflower margarine
3 large bananas, mashed
¼ teaspoon vanilla extract
2½ cups whole wheat flour

⅔ cup fine oatmeal
2 teaspoons baking powder
salt
l cup ground hazelnuts
2 tablespoons coarse oatmeal

Beat the date "sugar" into the eggs, and put aside for at least 10 minutes.

Beat the margarine until light, then beat in the bananas, a little at a time, and the vanilla extract. Add a little flour with each addition to prevent the mixture from curdling. Mix the remaining flour with the fine oatmeal, baking powder, salt and nuts, and alternately with the date "sugar" mixture, then fold it into the banana mixture.

Transfer the mixture to a greased 7 inch square baking pan, and level the surface. Sprinkle with the coarse oatmeal. Bake in a moderate oven, 350°F, for l hour until browned. Cool slightly in the pan, then turn out onto a wire rack to become cold.

OAT BREAD

MAKES TWO 1 lb LOAVES

1 ⅓ cups medium oatmeal **plus** extra for dusting
1 tablespoon oat bran and oat germ
1 ¼ cups skim milk **plus** extra for brushing
1 package compressed yeast **or** 1 package dry active yeast
3 tablespoons tepid water
1 teaspoon superfine sugar
3 cups whole wheat flour
salt
2 tablespoons sunflower oil

Soak the oatmeal and oat bran in the milk for at least 30 minutes. Blend the compressed yeast with the water, or reconstitute the dry yeast with the sugar and water. Leave in a warm place for about 20 minutes until frothy.

Stir the flour, salt and oil into the soaked oatmeal. Pour on the yeast liquid, and mix to form a stiff dough.

Dust your hands and a working surface with oatmeal. Knead the dough until smooth, then shape it into a ball, and place in an oiled bowl. Cover with oiled plastic wrap, and leave in a warm place for 1-1½ hours until the dough has doubled in size. Turn out the dough, and knead again for about 2 minutes. Divide it into two equal pieces. Place in two greased and floured 1 lb loaf pans, pressing the dough into the corners. Cover with oiled plastic wrap, and leave in a warm place until the dough rises above the tops of the pans.

Brush the tops with milk, and sprinkle with oatmeal. Bake the loaves in a very hot oven, 450°F, for 30 minutes until they sound hollow when tapped underneath. Cool slightly in the pans, then turn out onto a wire rack to become cold.

Variations

OAT BRAID
Divide each of the two pieces of risen dough into three. Shape each piece into a long roll or sausage. Take three of the strips, pinch the ends together, and braid the strips loosely. Pinch the other ends together. Repeat with the other three strips, place on an oiled baking sheet, cover with oiled plastic wrap, and leave to rise for a second time until doubled in size. Brush the tops with milk, sprinkle with oatmeal, and bake as above on a greased and floured baking sheet. Cool on a wire rack.

OAT ROLLS
Divide the risen dough into about 18 pieces. Shape into balls, then leave to rise as for the Oat Braid until doubled in size. Brush the tops with milk, sprinkle with oatmeal, and bake as above for about 20 minutes until the rolls are well-risen and sound hollow when tapped. Cool on a wire rack.

CHEESE AND HERB SODA BREAD

MAKES ONE 8 inch ROUND LOAF

3 cups whole wheat self-rising flour
⅔ cups fine oatmeal **plus** extra for dusting
1 teaspoon baking soda
salt
2 tablespoons sunflower margarine
2 stalks tender celery, finely chopped
1 small onion, finely chopped

1 small onion, finely chopped
1 tablespoon chopped parsley
or 1 teaspoon dried herb
1¼ cups buttermilk
milk for brushing
½ cup Edam cheese, grated
2 tablespoons rolled oats **or** jumbo oats

Mix together the flour, oatmeal, baking soda and salt, then rub in the margarine. Stir in the celery, onion and herbs, then pour on the buttermilk, and mix quickly to form a firm dough.

Dust your hands and a working surface with oatmeal, and knead the dough until smooth. Shape it into a 8 inch round loaf, and place on a baking sheet sprinkled with oatmeal. Score the top into eight segments, and brush with milk. Mix together the cheese and oats, and press onto the dough. Bake in a hot oven, 400°F, for 35 minutes until well-risen and browned. The bread should sound hollow when tapped underneath. Cool on a wire rack. Serve on the day of baking.

Note This bread is especially good with both soups and cheese.

POTATO BREAD

MAKES ONE 1 lb LOAF

1½ cups whole wheat flour
½ cup rolled oats **or** jumbo oats
2 teaspoons baking powder
salt
1 teaspoon paprika

½ cup cooked mashed potato
1 tablespoon sunflower oil
1 scant cup water
2 tablespoons medium oatmeal

Mix together the flour, oats, baking powder, salt and paprika, then beat in the mashed potato. Beat in the oil and water, then turn into a 1 lb loaf pan. Sprinkle the oatmeal evenly over the top, then stand the pan on a baking sheet, and bake in a very hot oven, 450°F, for 25 minutes until well-risen and browned. Cool in the pan, then turn out onto a wire rack to become cold.

Note This moist, spicy bread is good with a salad meal.

DATE LAYER CAKE

MAKES ONE 9 inch CAKE

½ cup date "sugar" (page 89)
2 tablespoons orange juice
1½ cups whole wheat flour
salt
6 tablespoons sunflower margarine
⅔ cup medium oatmeal
1 teaspoon grated orange rind

FILLING

2 cups pitted dried dates, finely chopped
2 tablespoons orange juice

Soak the date "sugar" in the orange juice for at least 10 minutes.

Meanwhile, prepare the filling. Mash the chopped dates with the orange juice, set aside.

Mix together the flour and salt. Beat the margarine until it is light, then beat in the date "sugar", and continue beating until the mixture is creamy. Gradually add the flour, oatmeal and orange rind, and mix with a fork until the mixture resembles coarse crumbs.

Spread half the mixture over the base of a greased 9 inch loose-bottomed cake pan, and press down well with the back of a spoon. Spread with the filling, and cover with the remaining crumb mixture. Bake in a moderate oven, 350°F, for 45 minutes until well-risen. Cool slightly in the pan, then turn out. Serve warm, if possible.

Note Serve with lowfat sour cream or yogurt as a dessert, or with coffee.

DATE MUFFINS

MAKES 16

½ cup date "sugar" (page 89)
⅔ cup lowfat yogurt
1 cup whole wheat self-rising flour
1 teaspoon baking powder
salt

½ teaspoon ground cinnamon
½ cup medium oatmeal
⅓ cup pitted dried dates, chopped
1 tablespoon sunflower margarine, melted

Stir the date "sugar" into the yogurt, then set aside for at least 10 minutes.

Mix together the flour, baking powder, salt, cinnamon, oatmeal and chopped dates. Stir the melted margarine into the yogurt and date "sugar" mixture, and pour this on to the dry ingredients, beating until smooth.

Spoon the mixture into 16 greased patty tins or muffin pans, and bake in a hot oven, 400°F, for 15-20 minutes until well-risen and light. Serve warm if possible, or cold on the day of baking.

APPLE SCONES

MAKES 10

3 pared cooking apples, cored and
chopped
1 tablespoon date "sugar" (page 89)
2 tablespoons orange juice
1½ cups whole wheat self-rising flour
⅓ cup medium oatmeal **plus** extra for
dusting
salt
½ teaspoon ground ginger

½ teaspoon ground cinnamon
3 tablespoons sunflower margarine
skim milk

TOPPING

2 tablespoons rolled oats
½ teaspoon ground cinnamon

Cook the apples with the date "sugar" and orange juice until they are soft, then beat to a smooth purée. Leave to cool.

Mix together the flour, oatmeal, salt and spices, then rub in the margarine. Add the date "sugar" purée, then pour on just enough of the milk to make a firm dough.

Dust your hands and a working surface with oatmeal. Knead the dough until smooth. Roll it to a thickness of ¾ inch, then cut into circles with a 2 inch round cutter. Re-roll the trimmings and cut out more circles.

Place the dough circles on a baking sheet sprinkled with oatmeal. Brush the tops with milk, and sprinkle with the rolled oats mixed with the cinnamon. Bake in a very hot oven, 450°F, for 15-20 minutes until well-risen and golden-brown. Cool on a wire rack.

Note These scones are delicious spread with more apple purée.

GRIDDLE CAKES

MAKES 12

2 cups whole wheat self-rising flour
⅔ cup fine oatmeal **plus** extra for dusting
1 teaspoon cream of tartar
salt

2 tablespoons sunflower margarine
½ cup currants
1¼ cups lowfat yogurt
⅔ cup buttermilk (approx)
oil for greasing

Mix together the flour, oatmeal, cream of tartar and salt, then rub in the margarine. Stir in the currants, then beat in the yogurt and just enough of the buttermilk to form a soft dough.

Dust your hands and a working surface with oatmeal. Knead the dough until smooth, then shape it into two circles each ½ inch thick. Cut each one into six wedges.

Cook the cakes in batches for 4-5 minutes on a hot, lightly greased griddle or in a heavy skillet until golden-brown on each side. Partly cool on a wire rack, and serve warm, if possible, or cold on the day of baking.

Index